When

Parenting

Backfires

When Parenting Backfires

Twelve Thinking Errors That Undermine Parents' Effectiveness

Daniel Bates, LMHC

David Simonsen, PhD

DB PRESS

Creative Endeavors That Matter

ISBN: 0997311501
ISBN 13: 9780997311501
Library of Congress Control Number: 2016902751
Published by DB PRESS, Vancouver, Washington

Contents

Introduction

> You are the bows from which your children
> as living arrows are sent forth.
> —Khalil Gibran[1]

L et's be honest. Parenting is hard. From the moment children take their first breaths, parents are faced with decisions and choices that no manual could ever fully explain. The life of a parent is filled with uncertainty, confusion and challenge. And to make matters worse, once you've figured something out about parenting you're faced with a new set of challenges as your child develops and changes over their lifespan. And If you do not have a strong support system from your family or a community, you're left with little help.

Under the best circumstances, parenting will be the most challenging thing you ever do. But, when your child rebels against you, or is diagnosed with a mental health disorder, or struggles with addiction, or has run-ins with the law, then you are faced with the fight of your life. The challenge of parenting your child well will push you to your limits. You may find yourself doing your best communicate in a mature way, but your child won't listen. They won't respond to discipline, they act out in public, or they embarrass you in front of your peers. So, what do you do in that situation? You could seek out parenting material and advice, and you are bombarded with parenting philosophies, discipline structures,

---

1. Kahlil Gibran, *The Prophet*, p. 8.

incentive schemes, and programs. It may feel like everyone has a different opinion about how to parent, and no one agrees. If only there was something out there that didn't focus how to parent your child, but who you are as a parent?

I (Dan) am a Licensed Mental Health Counselor who has worked with families in the justice system for the last 6 years. And I (David) am a Licensed Marriage and Family Therapist with a PhD in Family Psychology who has worked with families in the Juvenile Justice System for 16 years. Our collective experience and knowledge have lead us to this conclusion: *who you are as parent is far more important than what you do as a parent*. For, what you do flows from you are. A proverb from Frank Outlaw, the creator of Bi-Lo, echoes the notion of who you are influences what you do:

> Watch your thoughts, they become words.
> Watch your words, they become actions.
> Watch your actions, they become habits.
> Watch your habits, they become your character.
> Watch your character, for it becomes your destiny.[2]

What you *think* trickles down to every aspect of your being and, for the sake of our discussion, the destiny of who you are as a parent. This book is not so much about your child— although this book will help you be more effective in how you parent your child— this book is about who you are as a parent. And in order to examine who you are as a parent, it is necessary to examine and discover the impact of your *thinking* and beliefs.

Plato, the Athenian philosopher, recorded Socrates's famous saying "The unexamined life is not worth living." A parent who is not conscious about what they believe and think in regard to themselves, their role as parent, their relationship with their child,

---

2. Frank Outlaw, *What They're Saying*, 1977.

their child's role and who their child is, will not be as effective of a parent as they could be. The danger of parenting without examining your thoughts is that distorted beliefs and thinking will influence your words, actions, habits, and character, which then shape the outcomes you have with your child or children. Don't let unexamined thinking be the determinative force in your parenting. The process of exposing and examining the way you think as parents gives you the space to correct faulty thinking and make changes.

As a therapist (Dan), I see parents do the work of thought examination every day. It's not easy, and at times, it can be very uncomfortable. So much of your identity is wrapped up in being a good parent. You don't want to let your children down or incur the judgment of a critical culture that rarely gives parents a break. And as a result, you don't do self-examination. Yet, if you really want to be an effective parent, then you need to be willing to face the discomfort of self-examination. This is a lifelong project. It can't be done overnight. But there is hope. As you mature in your thinking, you will mature in your parenting as well, which will lead to better outcomes with your kids.

So, what to expect from this book? The first chapter establishes what thinking errors are. This will serve as the foundation for all that comes. In chapters 2-13, there are four sections: Thinking Error, Backfire, Correction, and Family Example. The first part of each chapter, "Thinking Error," examines a mistake parents often make in their thinking. This is an important part because the thinking error doesn't really look like an error. It may, in fact, not be a thinking error in most cases, but when it comes to parenting, it is. And I show you why.

The second part, "Backfire," explains not so much the *why* (as in the first part), but the *how*. How does the thinking error not work with your kids? How does the thinking error hurt you or lead your children to lose respect? Important questions, right? I think Backfire is a great word to use for this part of each chapter. Backfire communicates the idea of someone's efforts working against them.

In the third part of each chapter, "Correction," we (Dan and David) offer up ideas, based on our experience working with families, to help correct the thinking error. For purposes of efficiency and readability, the personal pronoun will be used without distinguishing if it is referring to David or Dan. Please don't mistake correction for a one- or two-step process. Correcting a pattern of thinking is a process. It's hard work unlearning an unhealthy or ineffective way of thinking and replacing it with a better one, but the relationship with your kids is worth it.

Finally, in each chapter we share a story of a family one of us worked with that exemplifies the thinking error and how they implemented the correction. The names, genders, ages, and relationships have been changed in order to protect the confidentiality of clients. No identifiable data has been used in the writing of this book. The stories are illustrative and generalized so that any parent can benefit from them.

We invite to you keep reading. Some of these thinking errors you'll be able to spot a mile away. And if so, good for you! That's something to celebrate. Instead of skimming, I suggest perusing those chapters to see if there are any new ideas you can add to your effective parenting. There will be other chapters about which you might think, "Why is this even in here? That's not a thinking error at all!" If you find yourself thinking that, hold on tight. That is the chapter you will want to concentrate on the most. It will be the most instructive because it is likely addressing a blind spot you have.

We encourage you to let this book do its work. Let down your guard and be open to the new ideas. As we've already said, the biggest risk you'll take is facing discomfort. But, when you take that one, it provides the opportunity for you to improve your parenting skills and your relationship with your kids. We think any effective parent is willing to take that challenge. Are you?

Chapter 1
What Are Thinking Errors?

When we are no longer able to change a situation…we are
challenged to change ourselves.
—Viktor Frankl[3]

If you were out hiking and came across a stream, would you immediately start drinking? What if the water was contaminated? If the water was questionable, you wouldn't drink, right? But, let's say you are parched and out of water, what do you do? Many hikers don't even worry about contaminants because they have filters, which take out the bad and leave the good. In the same way that hikers sift water through a filter, parents sift their experiences through a

A filter of ideas, like a water filter, allows you to identify and extricate what may be harmful and be able to keep what's good.

3. Viktor E. Frankl, *Man's Search for Meaning*, (Beacon Press Kindle Edition, 2006), 1409–1410.

mental filter. This raises the question, what is a mental filter and how do they work?

A mental filter is the way you interpret or understand the events in your life, the behavior of others, your own feelings and actions, and specifically for parents, your child's behavior. For example, if a parent believes their kid is intelligent and they come home one day with a stellar report card, the parent won't be surprised by that information. If the parent believes their child to be unintelligent, then the stellar report card will come as a shock to them. Two different responses determined by two different beliefs. The problem for parents is that sometimes our filters can be faulty. Information goes into the filter and distorted interpretation come out. That distorted interpretation of your child's behavior determines your response which will likely to bad outcomes. See how the process works?

Here's an of how faulty filters lead to unhealthy behavior. I once worked with a woman who left her abusive husband of seven years. It took some time, but she managed to land on her feet. Everything was going well when she met a man. They started dating and things were going well. However, whenever the new boyfriend raised his voice, the woman would shut down entirely. She was too afraid to speak out of turn and incur the wrath of her partner. Yet the boyfriend didn't intend to beat her, scold her or abuse her in any way. Eventually, he got tired of his girlfriend shutting down during conflict and left the relationship. This pushed the woman deeper into her shell.

So, what happened here? Is this a simple case of miscommunication that so many couples encounter, or was there something deeper going on? As we explored her failed relationship in counseling, my client discovered that what she interpreted as abuse in her new relationship may not have been abuse. Based on her experiences from the abusive 7-year marriage, she assumed that conflict in an interpersonal relationship meant she was wrong, she would be beaten, and she needed to be quiet to survive. Miscommunication and unresolved conflict was the result, but the root issue was a false assumption in the woman's mental filter.

This story illustrates the power of one's beliefs and patterns of thinking. The way you think is so important. What you think determines how you behave. What you think determines how you parent.

Good parenting is a combination of accurate, reality-based, value-based *thinking*, which leads to healthy *behavior*. If there are errors in your thinking, there will be errors in your parenting. No parent can be perfect, however, identifying the errors in your thinking arms you against the most common pitfalls that parents today make.

Discovering your thinking errors can be an uncomfortable process, and no one likes to admit to a mistake. Yet the potential benefits outweigh the disruption to our comfort. There is power in naming problems. That is why every single *Alcoholics Anonymous* meeting begins with "Hello, my name is...and I'm an alcoholic." In the same vein say with me, "Hello, my name is... and I'm a parent who struggles with thinking errors."

Chapter 2

You Scratch My Back, I'll Scratch Yours

The thing that impresses me most about America is the way parents
obey their children.
—Edward VIII[4]

With all the advancements we've made as a society in terms of technology, science, infrastructure, and medicine, you'd think our lives would get easier, right? In fact, life has only gotten busier and more complicated in the twenty-first century. Each advancement brings another burden. Juggling work, family life, social life, personal aspirations, social media, being always within reach through e-mail or smartphones— all these pulls of attention can tax a parent. With each duty on our plate, our stress level gets higher, and our energy for our children gets lower.

Stress and the Brain

Stress directs the majority of resources in our brain to areas responsible for primitive survival instincts. In survival situations,

---

4. Gyles Brandreth, *Oxford Dictionary of Humorous Quotations*, (Oxford University Press, 2013), 11.

you need survival instincts. If a tiger leaps out at you while walking in the jungle, by the time you're done thinking about the tiger, the danger he poses, and what you should do in response, he's already eaten half of you and is thinking about dessert. But let's say you are not in a situation of physical danger, but something stressful happens. If you do not have a strategy to effectively manage stress, you would likely respond in one of three ways: *fight, flight* or *freeze*. Typically, based on your personality, family of origin, the circumstances, and the personality of your child, you will usually respond in one of the three ways when faced with stress. So, do you usually fight back- fighting fire with fire? Or, do you run away and try to find escape? Or, do you shut down and withdraw? How you answer these questions has an impact on your parenting.

You may say and do things that you regret afterward, but have little understanding as to why you did what you did. "Why did I yell? Why did I immediately get defensive? Why did I perceive my child's question as an attack?" What keeps us alive in the jungle against the tiger sabotages us with friends, coworkers, and family members.

So how does your stress response affect you in a parenting context? Parents who are stressed often make their parenting decisions based on their exhaustion, not on rational thought or values. They will give in to their child's demand because it would take more energy not to. In fact, discipline becomes such a chore that parents will do anything to get their children to stop.

Without a strategy for managing stress, parents react to their kids instead of responding to them. What's the difference between *reacting* and *responding*? A reaction is acting without thinking. Responding is thinking before you act.

To illustrate the difference, imagine your child is whining loudly at the grocery store for some candy. You hadn't planned on buying any candy because you just bought food for dinner to make after shopping. But your child is onboard with the game plan and wants the candy. At first you ignore his repeated request for the candy, but he starts to cry louder and louder. Loud crying turns into a full-on temper tantrum. Other people are now giving you *that* look. What do you do? Stand your ground and draw more attention and embarrassment? Or, stop your child's whining by giving in? Maybe you buy a few candy bars for yourself and eat them all? That last question was a joke.

We have all been in that classic grocery store situation—feeling stressed, seeing all the eyes bearing down on us— there's little time to think so we go to our default ways of dealing with stress. If you were to simply react, you might give-in to stop the complaining. Or, you might respond and manage the irritation of your child's complaining and the embarrassment of the others attention. There are pluses and minuses with either way of dealing with the stress.

If you react and give in to your child's demands, the plus is that they stop complaining, people stop gawking at you, and maybe your child acts sweet towards you. The minus is that you can guarantee the next time you go to the grocery with your child, you will be having the same battle again.

If you respond by letting your child know they don't get something simply because they demanded to have it, the minus is that they will continue to complain. And people will continue to gawk and it will be an uncomfortable shopping trip to say the least. BUT, the plus is that you will see a sharp decrease in that type of behavior in the future because your child will implicitly understand that demanding doesn't work. Your child will respect you because you were consistent. And you can feel good that you stood your ground.

I hope you can see that responding to your child's bad behavior is far more healthy and effective than reacting. The question then becomes, how do I consistently practice responding to stress versus reacting to it?

Emotional Bank Account

You must be on your guard when emotional resources are low. If you are not, then you will react to your child than respond. Imagine that your energy, emotional capacity, and tolerance for stress is like a bank. Each stressor takes some of your emotional/energy resources from the bank. If there have been several withdrawals from the account, you have little energy to manage taxing situations. In other words, you won't be at your best. You make small concessions or bargains in your mind. "OK, if I give in now, he'll stop whining, and I can get the rest of my shopping done," or "If I let her go out, maybe she'll like me again." If you are always parenting from an emotional deficit with no way to manage stress effectively, you will find yourself settling. Settling for bad behavior. Settling for bad outcomes with your child. Settling for inconsistency.

> *In order to get what they want; our kids stress us to our breaking point.*

You must be a wise money manager of your emotional and energy resources. Because your bank account is maxed out, you give in to their demands. In other words, what you are doing is a form of bribery and bartering. *I scratch your back* by giving in to your demands *and you scratch my back* by behaving properly or at least stop behaving badly.

We make deals with our children instead of gently but firmly enforcing the standards we have already set. This establishes a bad precedent that children are acutely aware of. We give in to their demands in the hopes of getting good behavior from them. Or because we are needy and want approval from our children.

It is hard to argue against the effectiveness of bribery and bartering. Let's be honest. It works in the short term. But what if this was your go-to parenting strategy? How does this strategy work in the long run? Over time, parents rely on bribery and bartering more and more with the expectation that it will engender compliance and gratitude, but does it work?

Backfires

Family Example

Laura was a young woman in a middle-aged body. She liked to go out, spend time with friends, and stay out late at a club. But her fun was always stifled by the fact that she was a single mom. She loved her child, Mikayla, but her daughter was a wet blanket. This made Laura an impatient and demanding parent. She worked hard and wanted to play hard. She didn't want to be home to help Mikayla with homework, have consistent discipline, and reward her for good behavior. These were things she knew were right, but she felt "old" when doing them. When Mikayla acted out, Laura would get frustrated and send Mikayla to her father's house. He was a small-time criminal who sold drugs and on occasion used them. As a result of Mikayla spending time there, she picked up many bad habits.

Eventually Mikayla got in trouble with the law and was put on probation. She was forbidden to live with her dad. And was put on house arrest. Laura had little tolerance for bad behavior from her daughter. If she protested even mildly about an expectation, Laura would get exasperated and give in to her daughter's demands. She hoped, by giving in that Mikayla, in return, would stop the irritating behavior. This is where the bribe concept comes into play. Giving in was the *bribe*. The *bartering* was Laura's unspoken expectation that that Mikayla will then be grateful and stop the stress-inducing behavior. Laura was hoping that if she scratched Mikayla's back,

Mikayla would scratch her back. Unfortunately, it didn't work out that way.

Instead of "returning the favor" as Laura hoped Mikayla would, Mikayla learned that demanding got her what she wanted. So, Mikayla's behavior only got worse. Laura became so infuriated with Mikayla and tired of her parenting strategy not working, so she put Mikayla in foster care.

Sadly, the "You scratch my back, I'll scratch yours" strategy didn't result in the desired effect. This didn't work in Laura's situation and it doesn't work in general. Instead of the child becoming compliant and ingratiating when the parent gives in to their child's demands, your child learns that demanding gets them what they want. The child comes to expect that the parent will give in when they push their buttons. In the example with Laura and Mikayla, Laura giving in never resulted in a correction of bad behavior. All Mikayla ever learned was that her behavior was annoying, which resulted in mom giving in and Mikayla getting what she wanted. She never learned that her behavior was wrong, or that there were healthier, more respectful ways of getting what want. Bribery, bartering, and giving in are temporary measures at best. They are Band-Aids on a bigger problem.

Parents delude themselves into thinking that if they give in, it is a onetime thing, but they find themselves using the same strategy again and again. When they see that demanding works, children subconsciously create a strategy of pushing their parent's buttons. The bribe and barter method only increases the unwanted behavior from you child. So, what can you do as a parent to correct this problem?

Correction

Who's to Blame?

This may sound crazy, but it isn't your child's fault that you give in to their demands. Do not hold the fact that your kids use stress-inducing behavior to get what they want against them. Children, good or bad, test boundaries. It is how they are wired. In many cases, it is healthy. And is your job to lovingly and firmly enforce boundaries for your child, making it clear to them demanding will not get them what they want. Blaming will only create resentment. Furthermore, don't blame yourself. Stress, giving in, and wanting to avoid social embarrassment all happen to the best of us. Beating yourself up doesn't help anyone. The pattern described above is something every parent faces. But, what you do in response to that pattern needs to change. You need to develop better, more effective ways of handling stress. Acknowledging this provides you an opportunity to grow, not to wallow in despair. If anyone is to blame, it is the pattern of behavior. But there is hope; the cycle can be broken with hard work. So, what are the steps toward a solution?

1. Recognize the Problem: Change Your Thinking

Parents need to first recognize problem for what it is and take responsibility for their parent. Even though no one wakes up in the morning thinking, "I plan to sabotage my own parenting today by giving in when I'm overwhelmed" it happens. You must come to terms with this. Denial gets you nowhere. So, instead of denying the problem, or overly focusing on the problem, I want you to acknowledge that the problem exists, and then shift your attention to what needs to change.

Create a log of your week. Be ruthlessly honest and record each time you get overwhelmed and give in or want to give in. Change can't happen if you're not honest. Look to see if there are any patterns when this happens. Does it happen when you're multitasking? Does it happen in the morning or late at night? What leads up to it? What happens after? Can you identify a pattern?

When you have an accurate awareness of the triggers that lead you to giving it, then you can have awareness of what you are thinking and feeling, and make healthy choices. If you aren't aware, you will continue to follow the pattern and reap the negative results.

The fact that you get overwhelmed easily doesn't make you a bad person; however, it is an area of needed growth. Psychologists have categorized "getting overwhelmed easily" as *low distress tolerance*. The term means having a low capacity to withstand a stressful situation. Once you've reached a threshold, you make decisions, say and do things you wouldn't normally do or that you regret, such as giving in to your child's demands.

The solution to a low distress tolerance to build a *high distress tolerance*, which is the ability or capacity to effectively manage stress. So that when your child is pushing your buttons you can respond (not react) to them more effectively.

2. Build a Higher Distress Tolerance Level

In order to create high distress tolerance, you must first work on coping strategies to handle stress. Take a moment, with a journal and pen in hand, and imagine a stress-inducing situation with your child where you give in.

What am I feeling?

What triggered that feeling?

How do I normally respond when feeling that way?

What are the problems with how I respond?

If I could respond in a better, healthier way, what way would that be?

Working through these questions helps you gain awareness on what doesn't work and helps you identify what you could do differently. But awareness is only the first step. When you have an understanding of the problem then you need skills to help mitigate the stress.

Dialectical-behavioral therapy (DBT), created by psychologist Marsha Linehan, is a great resource for learning how extreme emotional states like stress can hijack our thinking and behavior in ways that hurt us and our parenting. Linehan has come up with several techniques that can help parents manage stress and anxiety in effective ways.

DBT has developed the technique of *radical acceptance*. This is a skill, applied to parents, with which the parent accepts the child's behavior for what it is. Parents learn to understand what is within their control and what is not. A whining and demanding child is not within a parent's control. How the parent responds, which can then shape the child's bad behavior, is within the parent's control.

Develop a *mind-body awareness*. Your mental and physical states are strongly connected to each other. Physiological arousal affects how you feel emotionally, and how you feel emotionally can affect your body. For example, when your child screams in the supermarket at the top of his or her lungs, your heart rate likely increases, you get hot in the face, your palms get sweaty, you start breathing faster, and your vision gets a little blurry. These are physical responses caused by an emotional reaction. Therefore, it is possible to calm your emotions through physiological techniques. DBT has a method called *Self-Soothing*. The idea is to soothe one of your five senses to ease emotional distress. For example: taste—eating chocolate, warm tea; touch—massage, pressure points, exercise; smell—candles, fresh air; sight—meaningful pictures, relaxing scenes; and hearing—calming music, a funny podcast.

Understand that you are the most influential person in your life, and the message you tell yourself is likewise the most powerful. We respond negatively or positively not because of what others say, but because of what we say to ourselves. Therefore, it is essential to develop the art of positive or realistic self-talk. *Self-talk*, simply put, is how we talk to ourselves. These conversations or messages are usually hidden, meaning that if they are inaccurate or needlessly negative, they cannot be challenged. Having inaccurate and negative messages that we tell ourselves throughout the day primes us to respond negatively to others.

If you do not build a high distress tolerance and teach them that demanding and irritating people to get what they want doesn't work, how will that affect their future career? Imagine your child as an adult believing that they get what they want when they demand and annoy others. They may approach their boss and demand a better schedule or higher pay. When the boss says no, your grown-up child may throw a fit, yell, and demand to get their way. It is likely they will lose that job as a result.

If you do not build a high distress tolerance and teach them that demanding and irritating people to get what they want doesn't work, how will that affect their intimate relationships in the future? If they want something from their intimate partner, so they use the strategy they learned while growing up— demand, irritate, intimidate— thinking that's how you get what you want. Either the other person refuses, resulting in the loss of the relationship, or they give in, which could lead to a co-dependent relationship.

3. Anticipate Stressors

Being forewarned of an upcoming danger or disaster can give you time to consider how to best respond. Therefore, I want you to assume that your child will behave poorly. Do not live in denial hoping the problem will just work itself out. The change needs to start with you, and then everything else will follow.

Ask yourself, what will produce the best long-term results when my child demands, whines, and pushes me to my breaking point?

Ask yourself, what standards am I reinforcing in how I respond to my child? Is the way I respond to my child the standard I want to set? Ask yourself, do I want my child to think "demanding gets me what I want"?

The hard truth is that all the disciplining you are bypassing now will be doubly needed later. This problem simply won't go away because you want it to. There are many kids who grow up dependent on their parents, not ready to launch, because their parents always gave in to their demands. And therefore, they have no concept of delayed gratification and hard work. They are entitled. So, ask yourself what values you are teaching your child, explicitly and implicitly. The *explicit values* are what we say; the *implicit values* are what we do. The implicit values you teach your child will have a greater impact than the other (I will say more on this in future chapters).

What you do—your actions, your behavior—is the most meaningful aspect to your parenting. Your words play second fiddle to your actions.

4. Responding Versus Reacting

Do you typically react to your child's triggering behavior or do you respond to their triggering behavior? In order to answer that question, you need to know the difference between a *reaction* and a *response*. As we discussed earlier, a reaction is action without thinking. A response is action you take after thinking. And what you think about is determined by your goals, values and strategy. So, let's work through each one.

What are the goals you have for your child?

What values do you want to instill in your child?

And, what is your strategy to motivate your child accomplish those goals and to teach those values?

When you have clear, established goals, it changes the way you respond to your child. For example, let's say you're in the grocery store and your child wants candy. They start crying and screaming to get it. First, do not give in. Then, think about a goal you have for your child. Let's say you want them to learn the skill of negotiation.

If your child is willing, you can negotiate with them regarding the candy. Ask your child, what are they willing to do in order to get the candy. Put the responsibility for *them* getting the candy on *them*, not on *you*. So, your child offers to do additional chores to get the candy. And you agree to those conditions. But, your work is not over yet. Then, you must keep your child accountable and check if they have met their end of the bargain. If your child followed through, then that is a positive option for them in the future. If they have not, then they lose the option of negotiating for candy in the future.

Negotiation incentives your child to get what they want, but not through whining and demanding. This is where the values come into play. You, as a parent and as a person, for example, value respect and patience. When your child demands candy from you, impatiently, that is a violation of your values for them. Do not reward this behavior with giving to their demands, thus reinforcing the opposite of your values. Rather, reinforce your child making respectful requests, done in a patient manner.

One of the greatest gifts we can give our children is responding with firm love in their worst moments. When they are acting out, this is when they need us the most. They don't need you to be angry, take things personally, or shut down. Instead, they need you to model patience and respect. Therefore, respond in a way that is consistent with your parenting goals and values, they will determine your strategy of how you will respond to their bad behavior. Don't allow stress or frustration to derail you.

Understand, when you start making positive changes in how you think and how you parent, your child may resist at first. It will be a baptism by fire; they will use every tactic available to get what they want at the most inconvenient and stressful times. Your first inclination will be to go to your default responses, but you must learn a better way of responding. This means you must retrain how you think and respond to your child following the steps laid out in this chapter.

Chapter 3

You're Always Breaking the Rules

Nothing of me is original.
I am the combined effort of everyone I've ever known.
—Chuck Palahniuk[5]

Lucinda, a single mom who works forty plus hours a week and has, for the last fifteen years, tried her best with her son, Max. They've always been close, but in his teen years, Max has started to change. He is independent and athletic, and he likes his freedom. He likes his freedom so much so, he spends most of his time outside of the house. And despite his natural charisma, he can be gullible at times. Unfortunately, Max involved himself with a group of friends who liked to

> *When Max did do something right, Lucinda was suspicious of it. She only saw what Max did wrong.*

---

5. Chuck Palahniuk, *Invisible Monsters*, W. W. Norton & Company, 104.

break and enter homes and steal expensive electronics.

Mom, unaware of what her son was doing with these "friends," became increasingly suspicious. Max had new clothes and new video game systems, but she knew he didn't have a job. So where did he get the money? Max would never give his mother a clear answer when she asked, or he would tell her, "Don't worry about it."

Eventually Max was caught and arrested. Mom was heartbroken, to say the least. Not only was he doing something illegal, for which she had to pay fines, but she was hurt most by his lies. She thought, "We don't have much, but if he had asked, I would have given him what he needed. Why did he do that? How could he do this to our family? How could he lie to me?"

From there, things only got worse for Lucinda and Max. Lucinda didn't trust anything Max said. When Max did do something right, Lucinda was suspicious of it. She only saw what Max did wrong. Every time he made a mistake, it brought back all the old feelings of betrayal. Max complained that all his mom ever looked at was his mistakes.

Lucinda feeling so distrust is understandable— it's hard to trust again after the bond of trust has been broken. It's hard to see the good in a person when they have betrayed you. Repeated breaks in trust push people to assume the worst about each other. For parents, when a child, time and time again, doesn't listen, makes the same mistakes, or willfully disobeys you, resentment builds. You may begin to doubt yourself as a parent if this parent continues, or wonder about the sanity of your child. The joy and vitality of your life and relationship runs dry. And if you let it, your child's chronic bad behavior shapes you define them. You've come to expect the worst from them. Another way of putting it is that bad behavior from your child creates an assumption or bias that you can't break away from. Therefore, it is important to examine not only your child's behavior, but also, your perceptions of your child's behavior, and how that too, may play a role the negative pattern unfolding between the two of you.

> *It is not true or honest to say someone is solely defined by their bad behavior.*

Identity

What defines a person? What they *do*, or who they *are*? It may be tempting to define the identify of your child based solely on their behavior. And, in the case of repeated disobedience, it may be even more tempting to define the identify of your child solely based on their bad behavior. More often than not, I've seen parents who face repeated disobedient behavior from their child make negative *interpretations* about the identity of their children.

What do I mean by negative interpretations? When your child acts out, a *negative inner dialogue* starts running through your head. "They are acting just like their father." "That liar has lied to me one too many times!" "This situation is hopeless; my child will never change or learn." It is important to understand these inner dialogues are not always accurate. They can be influenced by many different factors that may bear no relevance to your child. Things like past trauma, stress at work, or disagreement with a spouse or another family member can invade how you perceive your child's behavior if you are not aware of these outside influences.

For example, I've worked with parents who have made decisions pertinent to one child that are determined by the behavior of another child. And believe me, I have seen this blow up in the faces of many a parent. Or, for example, a parent loses their job and then takes out their anger and frustration on their child when they commit a minor misbehavior, this too can poison the well of the parent-child relationship.

Hopefully you can see, when a parent allows their vision to be clouded, when they make an attribution about the character and identify of their child based on unrelated factors to their child, the gears of change and the flow of relationship stop.

You must understand as a parent, children will react negatively to having their identity reduced to their bad behavior. In fact, most people respond negatively to having their identity reduced to one aspect. Why? Humans are multifaceted creatures. Our character is defined by patterns of behavior over time. We have stories. And to take only one aspect of a person's story, and defined them just by that, it is unfair and inaccurate.

It is not true or honest to say that people are solely defined by their bad behavior. And if you are doing this with your child, it needs to stop. You have *chosen* to selectively focus on the negative and ignore the other aspects of their characters.

Tunnel Vision

More than being inaccurate, negative inner dialogues may play a role in increasing the bad behavior of your child. How so? The stress from bad behavior pushes parents to their worst thinking and behavior. Imagine that you are a train, and the track is your life. As you're going along the track, you can see everything: forests, towns, cities, and rivers. However, when you enter a tunnel, your vision goes dark. All you can see is the light at the end of the tunnel. For all you know, the track could be missing, something could be blocking you, or there's a large hole near the end. In other words, you have no clue what's in the tunnel. All you perceive is what you can see. Granted, this is a weak analogy. The analogy of a horse with blinders works just as well. But it does help to illustrate a point. The stress created by the child's bad behavior bring the *negative inner dialogues* to mind. If that negative inner dialogues then becomes the running narrative for a parent perceives their child all the time, parents will only focus on what's going wrong. Like being in a tunnel, focus narrows what you can see.

A parent with a *negative focus* is suspicious of good behavior. And when the child misbehaves, it confirms the parent's bias. The more this bias is confirmed, the harder it is to see the child from another perspective. Sadly, for some parents, the broken trust and repeated bad behavior from their child is then used as justification for their own bad behavior. Parents will vent all their anger and frustration on their children when they've behaved badly.

Backfires

Reinforcing the Negative

When your child's bad behavior creates an overriding negative focus, your effectiveness is sabotaged in several ways. You may not realize it, but your child can pick upon your negative inner dialogue. They can sense it by the things you say, by the way you respond, and by the choices you make. And your negative inner dialogue will become theirs.

In the case of Lucinda and Max, Max made some serious mistakes, but Lucinda played a role in the continuation of his bad behavior. How? She allowed her negative inner dialogue to define her son's identity. He picked up on how mom perceived him, which he internalized. He began to see himself as his mom did, which then increased his acting out. He thought he was bad, so he behaved badly. His perception shaped his behavior.

So, what are some ways in which a parent's negative inner dialogue becomes their child's? Whatever you respond to gets reinforced. This may sound like a radical statement, but it's absolutely true. If you respond to your child's positive behavior, that is the behavior that gets reinforced. If you respond to your child's negative behavior, that is the behavior being reinforced. What behavior gets the biggest response from you? Over the course of a week, what does your child do that gets your attention?

Responding only to your child's bad behavior can create a negative cycle, a downward spiral. It's easy, like Lucinda did, to only see the negative after trust is broken and there has been betrayal. But to then expect bad behavior and to only respond to bad behavior undermines the parent because that reinforces the bad behavior. Negativity begets negativity. In other words, you reap what you sow. The child associates bad behavior with a response from the parent since the parent doesn't respond to good behavior.

The Limits of Perception

A negative focus can also affect your child's motivation. If you as a parent are always expecting the worst that can taint how you perceive good behavior from your child. You may respond with suspicion rather than praise when your child does something right. Overtime, your child may adopt a "Damned if I do, and I'm damned if I don't" attitude. This is what psychologists term as a *double bind*. And as parents, we want to avoid, as much as possible, putting our kids in double bind situations.

What is a double bind? A double bind is defined as a situation in which someone is faced with two irreconcilable demands. More specifically, in the context of the parent-child relationship, a double bind is a situation when the parent gives the child two expectations and to obey one is to disobey the other. In other words, it is no-win situation. Putting kids in double binds poisons the parent-child well, so to speak. Double binds build resentment and kill motivation. For example, when a parent teaches their child to have "a voice," to be "empowered" and "speak up for themselves," yet when the child speaks up for themselves and uses their voice *with* the parent and the parent shuts them down and scolds them for "backtalking," this is a double bind.

> *Whatever you respond to gets reinforced.*

Correction

Create New Inner Dialogue

The correction to the negative-focus cycle is not an easy one. But if parenting were easy, this book wouldn't be necessary. As the parent, you have to break the cycle of negative focus. That means, first, changing your negative inner dialogue.

If your child repeatedly behaves poorly, breaks trust repeatedly, and betrays you over and over, you must resist the temptation to define your child as untrustworthy and disobedient. Everything within you will want to dwell on the negative. But, you know that dwelling on the negative leads to the tunnel vision problem. Dwelling on the negative makes you more likely to notice the negative and less likely to notice the positive. This is not where you want to be.

You must force yourself to be observant of the positive. This is the second step in breaking the negative focus cycle. Even if you have to be creative in how you discover the positive actions and intentions of your child.

You have the choice to either perpetuate bad behavior by reinforcing your child with a negative perception or to purpose redirect your attention to the positive. In this regard, your child does not have the control. You have control in what you notice and pay attention to. You've allowed your child and their bad behavior control you long enough. You are going to reclaim control by noticing and praising the positive, even when you don't feel like it. What this does is to create a positive cycle in place of the negative one.

This requires you to look *past* bad behavior and look *to* what your child can become. You may have to pluck out the positive from their character with needle-nose tweezers, but no one person is truly all bad or truly all good. Even the worst of people have some *good* in them.

Even if your child has chronically done wrong, relentlessly praise when they do right. This can be incredibly hard to do since people generally are like turtles. When turtles sense danger, they recede into their shell for protection. When people are hurt, they put up barriers to self-protect. Don't let your self-protection sabotage your parenting.

When you can demonstrate your commitment to discovering and affirming the positive in your child, it builds confidence in your child. It lets them know that you believe in them. The value of believing in your child cannot be overestimated. This is the third step in breaking the negative focus cycle.

Believing in your children, seeing the best in them, or seeing what they could become, is like investing in a 401(k). You may not be able to cash in on it now, but it will pay off in the future. When parents can demonstrate their belief in what their child can become, even if their behavior is out of control, and all the evidence points to the contrary, it will plant a seed in their child. Because, as it has been said, perception is reality. Sometimes, reality is what we create. Our belief in someone can be bigger than the vices oppressing them.

Believe in your child. Love your children when they are unlovable. See the best in them when they cannot see the best in themselves. Your belief will create a template they can grow into. Don't let hurt cause you to reinforce their negative behavior.

Give Feedback Grounded in Behavior

It is my hope that you do not read what I am saying and then conclude one of two things. First, that I am suggesting you always be positive and never correct, discipline, or keep my child accountable. Or, because I am talking so much about a positive focus, I'm discouraging you to correct, discipline and keep your child accountable. I am saying neither.

This discussion does not negate the need for parents to correct, instruct, discipline and hold their children accountable. In fact, I regularly teach parents and encourage parents to do all the above. But, to do so with balance, and to do so with a purpose in mind, that is geared towards reinforcing the positive and investing in strengths.

Therefore, when you do discipline and give feedback to your child, focus on your child's behavior. Why do I recommend this? When you verbalize your negative inner dialogue. For example, let's say you catch your child in a lie. You think they are a liar and you call them that. Labels like liar are sticky. They stick your child identity. They shape your child's identity. This is a shame-based style of parenting and shaming children simply doesn't work and comes at a great cost. I discuss the problems with shame-based parenting in chapter 13.

Giving feedback on specific behaviors, using guilt for motivation, and offering your child reproof and correction is not somehow mean or unloving. That could not be further from the truth. But you need to embed your feedback in the frame work that you are correcting them because you believe they are better than how they behaved.

Family Example

James was a single dad. He and his daughter, Rose, had a tumultuous relationship. Even though she was eleven, she could pack a punch physically and verbally. Every time Dad met his daughter after school to take her home, Rose would walk right past him. Dad would wake up early every morning to make her lunch and write her a note of encouragement. He often found the notes crumpled in the garbage. Sometimes, after Rose would

> *Even though he didn't like Rose being in trouble at school, with the law or with him, he loved those rare occasions when she would let him into her world.*

act especially badly, she would warm up to Dad. It seemed like the only time they ever connected was when Rose was in serious trouble. James thought in the back of his mind, "Maybe she will

change, or maybe this is how our relationship will be from now on."
In spite of how bad things got, James still hoped he and his daughter
would have a good relationship. Even though he didn't like Rose
being in trouble at school, with the law, or with him, James loved
those rare occasions when she would let him into her world.
However, the moments of connection wouldn't last long. As soon as
he would feel like they were starting anew, Rose would become cold
and turn off again. With each attempt, James made to connect with
his daughter, Rose would react with increasing anger.

After a great deal of self-doubt, James finally took Rose to a
specialist. The psychologist diagnosed Rose with borderline
personality disorder; a disorder that makes it hard for people,
particularly girls, to form stable attachments with others. They tend
to push away those they love and then voraciously seek their
approval and love in no consistent manner. James was relieved to
finally have a term to describe his experience. But with that relief
came terror. He wondered if his daughter would always be this way.
He thought they were doomed to have a push-pull relationship. As
Rose got older, things progressively got worse. She was expelled
from school many times and put on probation as a juvenile
delinquent for fighting another girl. Everything seemed hopeless.
However, James never quit. He took his daughter to many
counselors, participated in sessions as often as he could, and worked
extra hours and at another part-time job to pay for her treatment.
And even though her rejections of him hurt, he never stopped loving
her. Every once in a while, James and Rose would connect. The
connection wasn't what surprised him though, it was when they
connected. He and his daughter were connecting outside of the
occasions when she got in trouble.

Over the coming months and years, Rose started going to school
more consistently. She got off probation. She stopped fighting with
other girls, and most important of all, she and her dad connected. It
was what Rose had secretly wanted all these years, but she didn't

know how to get it. And each time Rose got scared, she took all her fears of being rejected out on James. But through the tears and heartbreak, Dad was steadfast.

It was James's belief and hope in what his daughter could become that made all the difference. He disregarded all the hurt, rejection, ingratitude, and bad behavior. He loved her enough to look past those failures. His love outweighed his hurt. He didn't allow Rose's bad behavior to change his. His unshakable love created a different template for life that Rose could inhabit, grow into, and embrace.

Have a Strengths-Based Perspective

In order to break your child's negative cycle, you must first break your own cycle of negative perception. You must take on a strengths-based perspective. Look for the good, which in some cases may require you to get creative. Do this even when it's hard. This sends a powerful message to children even when they are behaving poorly. You are sending the message that you believe in them, you see that there is more to them than their bad behavior, and you are painting a future picture of what they can become.

Looking for strengths is different when looking for positives. What's the difference? Strengths-based perspective involves looking at the positive actions your child does and making positive attributions about their character. For example, when your child responds to your request the first time, as opposed to not listening and you having to repeat yourself many times, you can praise your child for their quick response and you can also assert that they are *efficient,* or *timely.* That may seem small, but it can double your returns when investing in your child.

Or, for example, a frustrated parent who had to offer an incentive to their child to get them to engage in family activities could have dwelt on how frustrated they were. But, when trying to break the negative focus cycle, noticed that their child was very conscientious of how much their favorite activity cost and expressed concern about it being too expensive an activity. This moment, one in which the parent usually would have complained or made a cutting remark to their child, chose to go down the strengths-based perspective and praise their child for being mindful about money. And that is a great quality since they will have to be mindful of money when they are an adult.

Your focus isn't just that they *did* something well, that is important, but what they did is an indication of *who* they are, in a positive sense. This is a reversal of the negative focus cycle. It is, for lack of a better term, the positive focus cycle.

Why Do You Do What You Do?

What is the goal of parenting? How you parent follows why you parent. So, ask yourself, what is the purpose behind each action you take as a parent? Is it to help your child grow into the person he or she can become and learn how to be a helpful, good, self-sufficient adult? Or do you do what you do because you want your child to like you? Are you seeking your child's approval? Thomas Phelan, psychologist and author, wrote in his book *1-2-3 Magic*, "Too many parents these days are afraid of their children. What are they afraid of? Physical attack? Not usually. What many parents fear is that their children won't like them."[6]

Effective parenting involves having a long-term focus instead of a short-term focus. What may work for the short term—or in the immediate moment—may be disastrous in the long run. You must ask yourself what the intended effect of your actions is. What are you hoping to accomplish with your discipline, rewards, or communication to your child?

---

6. Thomas W. Phelan, *1-2-3 Magic: Effective Discipline for Children 1–12* (Independent Publishers Group, 2003), p. 18.

Understand that the negative focus limits your vision. Remember the train in the tunnel analogy. Negative focus narrows your field of vision so that you are biased to dismiss the good and selectively focus on or emphasize the bad. This is wrong. It's simply not fair. Ask yourself, am I only paying attention to the negative? Does my focus limit me from seeing the good? Could my focus be painting a false picture of my child that will only reinforce the negative?

Chapter 4

I'll Lose My Authority if I Appear Fallible

Vulnerability sounds like truth and feels like courage. Truth and courage aren't always comfortable, but they're never weakness.
—Brené Brown[7]

There is strength in weakness. Many religious, philosophical, and wisdom traditions teach this truth. Poets wax eloquent, stirring up images of resilience and courage under duress. Singers and songwriters—from Pink and Destiny's Child to the Beatles and Queen—have belted out power ballads about surviving, going on, and falling down but getting up again. Self-help writers fill the shelves with how-to manuals about psychological, relational, and emotional resilience. We can safely say that, as a society, we like this idea of finding strength in vulnerability. But apart from liking the idea, do we really believe it? Do you believe that in vulnerability you find strength, acceptance, and courage? Or that vulnerability is weakness, and needs to be avoided?

For many of us parents, the answer is no. We do not model healthy and appropriate vulnerability with our kids. Why is that? In times of struggle, trial, and challenge, people often go into survival

---

7. Brené Brown, *Daring Greatly: How the Courage to Be Vulnerable Transforms the Way We Live, Love, Parent and Lead* (Gotham Books, 2012), 37.

mode. Survival mode may or may not be healthy. When times are hard, some like to isolate, oversleep, overeat, drink, and put up walls, and fear being seen by others. This is done instead of engaging in healthy behaviors to resolve a problem. As if this isn't bad enough, you have an audience. Your kids are watching every move you make. And, as I've said many times to the parents I work with, *your kids are aware of what is happening, but they do not understand what is happening.* Your kids see what you do, but they don't understand why you are doing what you are doing.

What you do now, will be what your kids will do in the future. So, when they see you struggle and then turn to substance use, binge-eating, unhealthy relationships, angry outbursts, obsessive authority, or shifting the blame, that's all they see. And, that's what is internalized. That becomes their model for how to deal with distress.

Sadly, when parents see their authority grounded in being perfect, their parenting skills get hijacked by fear.

Parents may never admit, to themselves or to their kids, to a vulnerability because they equate vulnerability with weakness or fallibility. And, if their kids see them as weak, then they will lose all authority or respect. So, they try to maintain a veneer of perfection or invulnerability. Sadly, when parents see their authority grounded in being perfect, their parenting skills get hijacked by fear.

For example, if your child knows you struggled in English during high school, does that encourage your child to do poorly in English? If you broke the law, struggled with substances, or ran away from home, do you think your mistakes will inspire them to do the same if they knew about your past? What if your child discovered you got pregnant in your late-teen years? Would you fear they'd use that against you?

Parents fear that past or current struggles disqualify or prevent them from being effective. This is a mistake. Past or current struggles can be the source of powerful and effective moments in our parenting.

Being open and honest about your mistakes can humanize you to your child. It can add meaning to your advice. It allows you to have empathy for your child's struggles. It lends relevance to your wise counsel. Yet parents undermine the power of their mistakes to empower their counsel and influence by avoiding their mistakes and presenting a facade of perfection.

Parents make the mistake of thinking they have to be seen as a superhero by their child. And if they lose their superhero status, the child's sense of well-being, security, and confidence will be lost. This couldn't be further from the truth. Parents tend to overestimate the impact of their actions in the wrong areas and underestimate in areas where they think they have little impact. *Your child's sense of security or respect for your authority is not grounded in how perfect you are, but in the quality of the relationship.* This will be explained later. For now, understand—to use a simple formula—that a parent who never makes mistakes and always has his or her business in order, does not always produce a stable and secure child.

Backfires

The pressure to present a model of perfection or failure-proof parenting backfires in several key ways. The fear of being authentic puts undue pressure on our kids to be perfect. Think about it. If all your kids ever see is you "having it all together," what does that mean when they don't have it all together? They will see their own struggling as an indication of failure.

What's even more damaging is the fact that you don't actually have it all together. You are putting on a confident face as you struggle and keep your feelings stuffed inside. Psychologist Sue Johnson calls this "silent desperation." Is suppressing and ignoring emotion something you want your child to emulate?

The fear of appearing weak or fallible also creates a false dichotomy for our children to accept. In other words, you are asking your children to play make-believe. Remember what I said earlier about kids being aware, but not understanding? Whether you like it or not, your children see more than you think they do. They know the chinks in your armor. Yet, when you never admit to a struggle and avoid vulnerability, it promotes pretense. The pretense that you, a person like everyone else who struggles at times, doesn't struggle. Over time, this erodes your children's confidence in you to be authentic. To put the shoe on the other foot, how would you like it if a person in authority over you—a boss, for example—had many imperfections apparent to all his staff, yet he pretended that he had none? First of all, you could never take that boss seriously. Second, you would eventually lose respect for him. Why would you put your kids in the same position?

This may be the saddest backfire discussed. Avoiding vulnerability during a struggle removes the opportunity for authentic discussion and relationship. *Challenges present opportunities for deeper relationships with our kids.* I'm not suggesting that you lay every thought on the lap of your children. There is an element of child-appropriate sharing that has to be considered here. But challenges open us up in different ways. We learn and share more about ourselves than we normally would. Why would you not share that with your kids?

Allowing your kids to see you struggle, in an appropriate manner, reinforces the idea that it is OK for them to struggle as well.

The greatest lesson your children will learn is not how perfectly you lived your life, but how resilient you were when struggling. That is the kind legacy you want to leave your kids.

And finally, when your children encounter a challenge, and trust me they will, they now have a positive model for how to endure, how to work, how to thrive in the face of obstacles.

Look at the benefits your child will lose out on if you avoid vulnerability. By pretending everything is OK, that you aren't struggling, you have effectively limited authentic connection between you and your child. You are teaching them to deny their feelings and to not reach out for support when they are struggling. These are lessons you cannot afford to skip teaching your child simply because vulnerability makes you uncomfortable.

Correction

The correction for this thinking error may seem counterintuitive. That is to say, the solution may seem contradictory at first glance. However, after further exploration and fleshing out, what at first seems paradoxical, contains a deep truth.

You worry that your child won't respect you or won't try hard if they see you as fallible. You may worry that your failures or weaknesses then become an excuse for your children's poor effort. Parents get caught up in this delusion that our failures will inspire our children to fail. But this is the wrong way to think.

Parents may also possess this thinking error because they do not know how to motivate their child, and they use their achievements as leverage. Where we have succeeded—or portrayed the appearance of having succeeded—we use it against our child. If our child has it easy in some way, a luxury we didn't have, or doesn't have to exert effort in a particular way that we did when we were younger, that is used to shame our child into better effort.

As parents, we ought to say, "I failed in this area, and my goal, as a parent, is for you to succeed where I failed." You're probably thinking, "Yeah, right, I would *never* say that to my child. I'm trying to show my child how to succeed, not give them a poor example." But this is hard because it requires humility.

When you can exercise humility, and be honest with yourself about your own challenges and weaknesses (shared in an appropriate way), it has, as I've said before, a paradoxical effect. Your children's knowledge of your past struggles, challenges, and weaknesses does not undermine your authority, their motivation, or their respect for you. In fact, it may even increase it. But how?

There is strength in our weakness. There is power in vulnerability. To quote Brené Brown again on parenting:

> By pushing away vulnerability, we turn parenting into a competition that's about knowing, proving, executing, and measuring rather than *being*. If we put aside the question of "Who's better?" and put out the yardsticks of school admissions, grades, sports, trophies, and accomplishments, I think the vast majority of us will agree that what we want for our children is what we want for ourselves—we want to raise children who live and love with their whole hearts.[8]

We need to ask ourselves, what do we want our child to become? Do we want them to be afraid of their own vulnerabilities or embrace them?

---

8. Ibid., 218.

When we can be authentic and vulnerable with our kids, they feel more comfortable in relating to us. They develop more respect for us because, like it or not, they can sense the insecurity and desperation. They can see the contradictions between our demands and character.

We delude ourselves into thinking our children are blind to our weaknesses, but that is naïve. Instead, be brave and humble and take ownership. Own your struggle. Own a challenge. Own the fact that you don't have the answer to a problem.

Vulnerability is the price you must pay in order for your child to grow. If you can be authentically vulnerable with your child, you are unleashing a powerful connecting force. Again, I caution you to make your sharing maturity-level appropriate. However, it is OK for your child to see you struggle.

So, what does this look like in practice? If you lose a family member, share your sadness over the loss. If you didn't get the job you were wanting, share your anger and frustration. If you are so happy that you're having another child, be excited; let your child see your joy. By expressing your feelings, you teach your child that feelings are normal and there is healthy way of handling them.

> *Vulnerability is the price you must pay in order for your child to grow.*

This is a powerful lesson to communicate to our kids. Many children today are afraid to struggle, so instead of trying anything hard, challenging, or taking a risk, they avoid the thing altogether. This does not build resilience.

Yet if you show your children *how* you work through a challenge, you give them a tremendous gift.

The *way* you cope with stress, anxiety, depression, and competition provides an example of how your kids can work through problems in a healthy way. For example, if you have a problem at work, and you enlist coworkers, mentors, and supervisors to help you, you just used a skill. You had the courage to request support from a network of people at work. The alternative is that you use no skill; that is, you don't share your struggle, you don't ask for help, and the problem never gets solved. Therefore, by showing your child what skills you used, how you thought through the problem, didn't give up when things got hard, and how you enlisted support during a challenge, your child can then learn from you. They will benefit from those skills they learned from watching you for the rest of their life.

And finally, if you can be authentically vulnerable with your child, you are showing them how to be emotionally intelligent and resilience. Challenges and struggles won't intimidate your son or daughter to the point where they are crushed. They know they can get through a hard time because they've seen it done. Resilience will not be an abstract concept. They will have firsthand, experiential knowledge of how to work through challenging times. This will increase their confidence and bolster their willingness to take something on that they previously thought impossible.

Family Example

Making these cognitive changes isn't impossible, even though it may feel that way. Take Jim and Elizabeth for example. Jim is the father of Elizabeth, and it would be an understatement to say their relationship was "conflicted." Their fights would affect the entire household. Jim was, as he described himself, "old school." He valued respect and had high expectations of his children. If there was a conflict or a decision to be made, or one of the kids raised an issue about the chores, Jim would overpower the other person. Warfare and power was his conflict-resolution style.

Most of the family knew that when Jim was upset or unhappy, look out. Most the time, the family would acquiesce to Dad, except for Elizabeth. When he would try to overpower her, she would fight back. And they would get stuck in power struggles. And when they fought, there were fireworks. Things were thrown, and doors were slammed. Family members who were not involved barricaded themselves in their rooms.

Things got so bad that Elizabeth began to disregard the rules entirely, not just the ones she thought unfair. She resented Dad for begin stubborn and a bully. As time went on, she felt more and more disconnected from the house. Eventually, she started running away and engaging in risky behavior like having unprotected sex with men she didn't know, getting intoxicated, and stealing cars. Dad interpreted Elizabeth's behavior as a rebellion against him, but everyone else could see it was her cry for help.

When I started working with this family, tensions were high. Yet as I worked with the family, I could access the family's softer feelings. I asked how Elizabeth's dangerous behavior affected the family, and surprisingly, Jim shared how scared, worried, and afraid he was for her. The extreme nature of his daughter's behavior shook Jim up. Elizabeth wasn't just rebelling, she was self-destructing, and Dad couldn't ignore that. He had to confront the reason why she was doing what she was doing. This was a vulnerable position for him to be in. He didn't like feeling what he perceived as weakness. But when Dad shared his more vulnerable feelings, this broke down a barrier in his daughter. She began to cry inconsolably. For her, seeing her dad hurt, cry, and show his sadness overcame her anger and bitterness.

They started communicating authentically and compassionately. Elizabeth felt sad and ashamed by the risky behavior she was engaging in. But she did what she did because she felt like she had no voice in the house. Dad overpowering her voice left her feeling disrespected, unloved, and disconnected. She felt like she had no connection outside of fighting. She courageously gave this feedback to her dad, and he listened. At several points, she thought he would fight back, but he didn't. He realized it was more important to listen to his daughter than to be right.

Dad shared that the kind of relationship he had with his father was similar to the one he had with his daughter. When he looked at her, he saw a lot of himself: strong-willed, intelligent, and stubborn. They were both fighters. He also shared that he rebelled in much the same manner as Elizabeth. But for the first time, he saw the impact of that rebellious behavior from the other side. He realized how much hurt and love he felt for his daughter. He was so fired up about her behavior because he was so invested in his relationship with her. This vulnerability, this display of "weakness" allowed Elizabeth and Jim to connect in a meaningful and positive way. They were able to negotiate more positive ways of communicating, decision-making and conflict resolution. Elizabeth felt like she had a voice and a place in the family. Dad felt like he had his daughter back.

When it came time to end therapy with the family, I asked Jim what he thought of his vulnerable sharing with his daughter. He said that the old dad, the one who existed before therapy started, would have thought that vulnerability was for "sissies." But the new dad saw that if he had not been vulnerable with his daughter, he would have surely lost her. He said *the price was too high to pay for not being vulnerable.* I asked him what he thought about making vulnerability an ongoing practice with his daughter and his family. The new dad recognized that vulnerability was a needed daily aspect of family life. They could not survive without it. He knew that being vulnerable was not a onetime thing. Vulnerability was what got them to where they were now—connecting in a positive and meaningful way—and it was what would help them continue growing.

Chapter 5

Perfection Is Progress

Seeking and blundering are good, for it is only by seeking and blundering we learn.
—Johann Wolfgang von Goethe[9]

What is one thing that Tiger Woods, the Williams sisters, Yo-Yo Ma, Oprah Winfrey, and Richard Feynman have in common? They were all pushed by their parents or grandparents to be the best from a young age. The topic of parental demands and expectations raises a host of questions for which parents struggle to find answers. For example, how much pushing from parents is too much pushing? How much pushing is too little?

To one degree or another, most parents want their children to be the best. Even if a parent doesn't desire this, there is feel pressure from the culture for parents to push their kids in athletics, academics, and extra-curricular activities. Parents may also put high expectations and demands on their kids after trust has been broken. Whatever the context, the demand for perfection creates problems for both parent and child.

Parents may think, "If I don't push my child to perfection, I'm doing them a disservice." The pressure parents feel then becomes the pressure their kids feel. And if the response to pressure is not

---

9. Carl C. Gaither, *Gaither's Dictionary of Scientific Quotations*, (Springer, 2012), 1156.

managed in a healthy way, it can become the consuming focus of the parent-child relationship. Parents may feel guilt when they're not constantly pushing their kids. Children may feel their parent's expectations are too rigid and unfair.

That isn't to say putting high expectations, demands and pressure on our kids is wrong. But the reasons *why* you push your children are just as important as *how* you push your children. You may feel that your child's performance reflects on your parenting. And so, there may be an element of ego involved when it comes to why you place demands on your kids. Do you see the connection?

If you determine the quality of your parenting based on your child's behavior, athletic or academic performance, then your parenting is about you and not your child. It's about your ego and proving to yourself and others that you are a great parent. This is a dangerous foundation for your parenting.

If you push your child for the purpose of building up your ego, your child can sense that. Over time, it is likely your child will grow to resent you. Even when you push your child for their benefit, they will not like the pushing. But if they can sense that it's done for selfish purposes, it will turn them against you.

In the area of trust, parents demand for perfection after bad behavior can lead to disastrous results too. If a child has misbehaved in terms of breaking trust, violating the law, damaging property, or hurting someone in the family, parents may be tempted to create unusually high standards in response. Parents may be unaware that they are doing this. The thinking follows as such: because the child damaged the relationship, they own a relational debt. For the child to regain what was lost, they have to pay back what they owe and extra.

Whatever the context, when parental expectations and demands are not done for the right reasons, in the right way, they can backfire miserably.

Backfires

Regarding performance, parents can be guilty of "shifting the goal post." What do I mean by that? When your child accomplishes a goal or milestone, if no acknowledgement of the achievement is given, motivation is killed. It is important to acknowledge what our kids do well. If we only focus on what they did wrong or what the next goal is, they will never feel the motivation given by victory.

High demands and expectations without skill development, encouragement or the feeling of a win will lead to resentment.

I'm not suggesting parents never give critical feedback. But pushing must be balanced with supporting. I've worked with many parents who are comfortable with pushing, but get nervous when it comes to supporting. They feel that offering support encourages weakness, or doesn't push their kids to perfection. This, I believe, is a serious misstep. Why?

Take losing weight, for example. We have all been there. It's the beginning of January. We have indulged over the holidays, and we cannot fit into our jeans. Time to go on a diet! New Year's resolutions are made. We download the weight loss app, pay for the gym membership, and write blogs about how motivated we are. And after all that, within two weeks we have completely failed. Why does this happen?

Too big of a goal with no rewards attached to milestones kills motivation. In other words, you need to break the goal up into smaller attainable goals. The bigger the goal, the more chunks you will need to break it up into. Breaking down the goal into bite-size pieces works best because it gives you the feel of a win on completion. That feeling of a win keeps your motivation up.

So how does breaking down big goals into smaller ones help you with parenting? Giving your child a large goal can be overwhelming. Especially considering that your child isn't equipped with the life skills to know when they need help, to schedule time to work on goals, to break the goal into smaller pieces, and to practice self-discipline. These are skills you likely have, but your kids don't.

Skill Building

So, when your child struggles with achieving a goal, that isn't the time to double down on your pushing. Their lack of perfection is an indication of a character flaw. It is information that the goal may not be attainable, therefore the goal needs to be rethought. Or, that your child doesn't possess the needed skills to accomplish the goal.

Think of failure as a "skill development" issue. You, as a parent, wear many hats, so put on the "teacher" or "coach" hat and dive into skill development by teaching your child how to break down large goals into smaller, attainable goals. Show them how to see problems not a sign of weakness or defeat, but an opportunity for growth as any good teacher or coach would.

This will eventually lead to burnout, and your child will feel defeated. It will also have a negative effect on your relationship. High demands and expectations without skill development, encouragement or the feeling of a "win" will lead to resentment. Demanding perfection is exhausting on the part of the person making the demands and on the person of whom the perfection is demanded.

If you don't do this, you run the risk of demanding too much for too long. I've seen many parents position themselves in one extreme or another. Either, they offer no support when their child is struggling, which can lead to the child feeling defeated, demotivated and helpless.

Failure, the Gateway to Learning

The other extreme is a parent who takes over when their child is struggling. This also leads to unwanted outcomes in that the child becomes dependent on their parents to do the work for them or have the solution. As opposed to becoming self-sufficient, and learning to problem solve.

You also must consider whether demanding perfection from your child is poisoning the well. What do I mean by that? By demanding perfection in a strict and/or harsh way, your child won't *learn from their mistakes*. Instead, your child will *learn to fear mistakes*. Think about it—fear of mistakes totally undermines learning and completely eradicates courageous risk taking. What if Steve Jobs had been too afraid to create the first affordable personal computer? He took a huge risk that easily could have failed. But he did it anyway. And in fact, the road that led to the 1984 Macintosh— one of the best-selling computers of all time— was paved with failure. The Apple III and the Lisa Project were both massive failures. But instead of giving up after failure, Jobs learned from his mistakes which built the foundation for future successes.

Foundation for Self-Concept

Parents who demand perfection often connect success or failure with their child's self-concept. Self-concept is the collection of fundamentals beliefs about oneself. For example, people sometimes describe themselves as traditional or progressive, and as fighters, hard workers, or persons of faith. These are labels that express their idea of themselves. Self-concept can either be a hindrance or a help.

When you connect failure to a child's self-concept, failure is utterly crushing. This is not what you want as a parent. You want your child to be resilient, to take courageous risks regardless of the outcome. And then, as Steve Jobs did, learn from those mistakes in order to make progress.

Perfection is an illusion. It doesn't exist. Someone else can always do it better than you. And most important, perfection sucks the joy out of life. So, you have to ask yourself, is perfection worth it? And if perfection really is an illusion, what are your *real* reasons to demand perfection from your child? Is pushing your child really for their benefit or for some other reason? More on this in the next section.

Correction

The *reason* why we push our kids is just as important as *how* we push our kids. Pushing our kids toward becoming their best selves is not altogether a bad thing. In fact, I think we are doing a disservice if we have no demands or expectations of them. But the goal is to find a nice balance of expectations and support. Therefore, it is essential to understand your reasons for pushing your kids. If your reason for pushing is in their best interest, then you will likely find a balance between expectations and support. If it isn't in your child's best interest, then the selfish or unhealthy reasons will lead you to imbalance. For example, you push your kid because it feeds your ego or something like that, then you will likely err on the side of demands and expectations and neglect your child's need for support. And when they don't respond to your pushing or meet your expectations, it's devastating to your ego. This is far more crushing than the less intense disappointment of your child not responding to a demand successfully. Therefore, push your child in the right way for the right reasons.

But how can you do this? The solution is to invert the thinking error. Huh? Instead of *perfection is progress*, adjust your thinking to *progress, not perfection*. This way of thinking puts the onus on *growth versus achievement*. That means, whenever your child makes steps towards a goal, although not perfect, you will praise and affirm that progress. When your child has broken trust, and they are attempting to rebuild trust, albeit imperfectly, praise and affirm their imperfect progress. When your child does 5 annoying, disobedient, and frustrating things, and then does 1 thing right, praise and affirm that 1 positive thing. *Don't let the negative negate the positive.*

We need to understand as parents *what* we give our children is not as important as *who* we give our children. Confused? You may not realize it, but every day, you give your son or daughter a piece of yourself. Who you are matters. The kind of person you are informs your parenting. You will read this idea over and over again in this book, but it's worth repeating: be the person you want your kids to be. And, as it turns out, a secure parent-child relationship is one of the most significant things parents can give to their children. If that's true, then it changes the choices we make as parents. There will be times that you may choice relationship over your child achieving a goal. There may be times your child will require a great of support, and then, at other times, they will require very little. This requires you to be skilled in the art of parenting, not the science. You may have to choose your battles, and lose a few in order to win the war.

The Importance of Attachment

When studying attachment—the relational bonding between people—developmental psychologists have discovered that children who have a secure attachment with their parents fare the best in life. They have self-confidence, do well in school, go on to have loving relationships, and earn more money as adults. To reiterate, the absolute best thing you can give your child is a secure relationship with you. Brené Brown quoted Joseph Chilton Pearce in her book *Daring Greatly*: "What we *are* teaches the child more than what we say, so we must *be* what we want our children to become."[10]

I suggest two goals for parents who want to be effective: prioritize the relationship you have with your child, and be an example to your child. Demonstrate the personal qualities you would like them to possess. For example, if you treat yourself with respect, your child will see that and learn self-respect. If you treat yourself with compassion, your child will see that and learn self-compassion.

If we demand perfection from ourselves—religiously beating ourselves down and having no joy in life—so will our child.

> *Word and deed must align in order to positively influence your child.*

Mahatma Gandhi once said, "Be the change you want to see in the world." I say to parents, "Be the change you want to see in your child." Lead by example. If you encourage your child but beat yourself down, your words lose their power. Word and deed must align in order to positively influence your child. Before trying to make a change in your child, make the needed changes to yourself first.

For the next week, instead of demanding perfection and then beating yourself or your child down with negativity, try changing your self-talk. When you encounter struggles or failure, tell yourself, "There are no mistakes, only feedback." This creates an opportunity for you to learn from your actions.

---

10. Brené Brown, *Daring Greatly*, p. 217.

With every failure, crisis, let down, or loss is an opportunity for growth and learning. However, this largely depends on one's perspective and thinking. Author Gary Thomas is well known for his books on the spiritual journey. However, it took over nine years and submission to over 150 publishers to get his first book into print. That's 150 failures per one victory. But getting that first book published launched a very successful writing career. Failure is not the end of the road; it's a bump in the road. Within each failure are valuable lessons for success. But many miss these lessons because their thinking is wrong. Change your thinking and you change yourself, which in turn, will change your child.

Family Example

I worked with a family in which the mom was a very powerful figure. Her name was Sue, and her son's name was Alex. She came from a long line of strong mothers, the kind of mothers who expected a lot out of their kids. During one of our initial sessions, I asked Sue about her mother. Her demeanor became downcast, she sat up a little stiffer in her seat, and she said she did not have a good relationship with her mom. Her mom always focused on what she was doing wrong. She never affirmed her; she never showed love or affection.

This relationship, unbeknown to my client, affected her parenting. The way she parented her son was almost identical to the way she was parented. Yet Sue couldn't see that. When I asked Sue about Alex, she gave me a laundry list of what he was doing wrong. In her mind, I wasn't there to help her or even the family; I was there to help fix her son.

Alex, as you can imagine, had a different opinion. Believe it or not, Alex cited complaints about his mom similar to the ones Sue voiced about her mother. Alex shared that his mom only saw problems and negatives. She never showed him affirmation or encouragement, or made overt or even subtle displays of love or affection. When he was struggling with a problem, Sue went into "lecture mode." She blasted him with questions, solutions, and exhortations on what he ought to do. Her pressure was overwhelming for him. She relentlessly pushed him to be perfect. And the result was almost always the same. Alex didn't bring problems to Mom anymore; he avoided her at all costs. If Alex was struggling with homework, he didn't seek her out for help. If Alex was having an issue at school—with a teacher, a fellow student, or his schedule—he refused to seek Sue out. He made every effort to avoid her.

Alex's avoidance only served to increase Mom's frustration and engagement with her son. They were locked in this push-pull cycle. Mom would pursue, and Alex would distance. Tensions built up from this negative pattern, and then things exploded. They would yell and scream. Alex would accuse Sue of being an overbearing, negatively focused, cruel mother. Mom would point out all the flaws in Alex, bring up every low grade, every perceived example of laziness, lack of effort, or disobedience. Things even got so bad that Alex spent a month with a trusted family friend to give the family a cooling-off period. Sadly, this managed to temporarily help but did nothing to solve the family's repeating negative pattern.

This was about the time I started working with the family. One thing I discovered early on was that Mom pushed her son to meet her high standards because she really cared about him. Her pushing was evidence of her investment in his future well-being and success. In fact, her problem was that she cared too much. I shared this observation with her—that her investment in her son making the right choice every time was so great that her approach inevitably undermined her efforts. That is to say, she was shooting herself in the foot. When she pushed, lectured, and drove hard on her son to be perfect, it actually had the opposite effect. Her approach led to Alex shutting down. His motivation dropping, and his performance bottomed out. Most important, their relationship was taking a big hit.

That last point really sank deep. Mom shared that she was hurt when Alex didn't seek her out for help but avoided her. She wanted a positive and close relationship with him. I shared with her that there might be a way that she could restore her relationship with her son and still achieve her goals for him. Needless to say, she was all ears.

I told Mom that her thinking was characterized by the axiom "Perfection is progress," meaning that she only responded positively to perfect performance from her son. And when he didn't perform perfectly, she made every effort to correct the mistake. She would lecture, nag, and take over. The problem with this line of thinking was that no one is perfect. Perfection is an illusion. It simply doesn't exist. So, if she made perfection her expectation, she was setting herself and her son up for failure because she was demanding of him something that no one could achieve.

Also, people aren't motivated by the negative. People are motivated by the positive. And this was evident in Alex's responses to Sue's pushing. Every time she pushed, his

> *The problem with this line of thinking is that no one is perfect. Perfection is an illusion. It simply doesn't exist.*

performance and motivation took a big hit. Alex felt like he was "damned if he did, damned if he didn't." He felt like his good behavior, successes, and achievements were never recognized or good enough. And when he made a mistake or misbehaved, he was lectured and punished. This led him to feel like it didn't matter what he did. He also didn't care about what mom thought. I pointed out to Sue that there were so many wise things to share with her son that could really benefit him, but his ears were closed to her influence because of her approach.

And most important, kids excel when they have a secure and positive relationship with their parents. If kids have an insecure or avoidant attachment, their performance in school and in sports drops, and their health and overall well-being suffers. One of the best things parents can do to ensure better health, motivation, and performance in almost every area of their child's life is to have secure attachment with their child. Sue would have to make choices about how she responded to Alex that built up the relationship and didn't always solve the problem or guarantee the best grade. It was more important for her to be there for Alex—to be his supporter, guide, safety net, and listener—than to make sure he did everything the right way.

In order to accomplish these new goals, I suggested Mom replace "Perfection is progress" with "Progress is perfection." With this new way of thinking, I wanted her to look for signs of progress from Alex. So every time he improved his grades, even if it wasn't a perfect score—recognize and praise. Every time Alex was quicker to respond to a request from his mom to do a chore—recognize and praise. In other words, I wanted mom to be on the lookout for the positive strides Alex was making. With trial and error, Mom tried out my suggestion. Over time, the better Sue got at noticing the positive and praising Alex for his efforts, the more she saw improvements in his motivation, confidence, and self-esteem.

Most important, their relationship improved. Alex no longer felt like his mom was hounding him all the time. He felt like she was his supporter. He no longer avoided her and even sought her out when working through an issue. Mom felt better too. When she noticed a positive action, she felt positive. In other words, acting positive made her feel positive. This allowed her to show and express love in more obvious ways to Alex. In turn, he felt more comfortable around mom. He shared more with her and was receptive to her feedback and influence. Mom shared with me that at first, she thought my suggestion was crazy. And she admitted that many times in the beginning she slipped into old habits. Or she felt like her noticing and praising made no difference with Alex. But over time, the changes in her thinking paid off. She had the relationship she had always wanted with Alex.

Chapter 6

I Love You Conditionally

Being deeply loved by someone gives you strength,
while loving someone gives you courage.
—Lao Tzu

Robert and Sandra were two loving and caring parents. They met in college, dated, and married shortly after graduating. After that, Robert went on to become an engineer on the East Coast. The couple started building their family with the birth of their daughter Anne. She was the model child—not fussy, generally happy, compliant, and appreciative of her parents. Robert and Sandra enjoyed parenting; Anne always obeyed, did well in school and aspired to be engineer like her father. All was well with the family until they had their second child, Adam. From the start, Adam was willful. When Robert tried explaining simple things like tying shoes, washing dishes, or playing catch, Adam always wanted to do it his way. He was easily distracted and had a hard time paying attention in school. The relationship between Adam and Sandra was especially rough. When Adam was disrespectful, Sandra was so hurt she would pull away and shut down. There would be long periods of silent tension in the home. However, Adam was so distractible, he'd forget the hurt he just inflicted on his mom and go in for a hug. Mom would pull away, not speak, and busy herself with other things. The two resented each other. The attempts on both sides for connection became few and far between.

As time went on, Adam started improving. His grades picked up, and the arguments decreased. Mom felt more at ease around Adam, and their relationship began to grow. But these "good" periods of time were short-lived. Adam went back to his old behaviors, and Mom became cold again. Sandra often contrasted Anne to Adam, exclaiming in frustration, "Why can't you be more like your sister?" This only made things worse. Adam behaved as he did before, acting badly and then reaching out to Sandra for connection, and she would pull away. Adam began to notice that when he behaved well, he felt like she loved him, but when he behaved badly, Mom was cold and distant. And neither one of them was willing to change.

> *He realized his mom didn't love him for who he was, she loved him for what he did.*

Hopefully, after reading the first half of Sandra and Adam's story (more on them later), you are able to pick up on a *relational pattern*. Mom's love and affection were offered if Adam behaved well. Adam realized this and grew to resent his mom. He felt that she didn't love him for *who he was*, she loved him for *what he did*. This completely demotivated Adam from trying to earn Mom's love. They were both trapped by this relational pattern. Neither one got their needs met.

Conditional Love

Sandra couldn't see outside of her own experience. She was only offering relational connection, support, and love for Adam when he behaved well. Otherwise, she was cold and distant. She would shut down. Reading this on paper she might seem cruel and coldhearted, but you'd be surprised how many parents do the same to their kids to one degree or another. You may even be surprised that this relational pattern has possibly crept into your parenting as well.

How could this be? Simple—it is human nature. It is hard to love someone when they've hurt you or acted badly— it's a natural response is to recoil when in pain. The reaction to withdraw connection is similar to a slug's response when touched. When a slug's exposed body is touched, it recedes into its shell until it feels safe. Many parents do the same. When parents are hurt, angry, disappointed, or in pain, they retreat to a place of safety. There's nothing wrong with wanting to recover after being disappointed or hurt, but a danger must be recognized. The danger is when a parent remains in that safe place and doesn't ever come back.

In the case of Sandra and Adam, she was understandably hurt by Adam's behavior. Her response was normal; she withdrew to a safe place to recover. The problem was that she wouldn't come out of that place of safety. She would ignore Adam's attempts to reconnect. This soured their relationship. Adam's bids for connection slowly decreased when Mom wouldn't reciprocate.

But there's another side to this thinking and that is some parents think they are helping their kids by doing withholding relational connection. The thinking goes like this: "My child has hurt me, behaved badly, or made a poor choice. Instead of giving my child connection with me, which will show approval for that bad behavior, I will instead remove the relational connection so as to motivate them to regain it through good behavior."

As you can see, there are two elements involved in this sort of thinking. First, the parent is punishing the bad behavior by removing the relational connection. Second, the parent is trying to motivate the child by providing the opportunity of relational connection as a reward for good behavior.

You may be wondering what's wrong with thinking that way. Keep reading!

Backfires

Trying to motivate your child to behave well with the rewards of relational connection will eventually backfire in disastrous ways. If attempts to connect are repeatedly rejected, the relationship loses its appeal for the child. Children become unmotivated and resentful of the parent. If you offer connection as the proverbial carrot for good behavior, you haven't increased desire for the relationship, you've decreased it.

> *Love is not a bargaining chip when it comes to parenting.*

John Gottman, a noteworthy psychologist and relationship researcher at the University of Washington, has discovered when bids for connection— his term for one person's attempt to relationally connect with another— are rejected, it decreases likelihood of future bids. To put it another way, if someone knows they will be rejected when they put themselves out there, they are less likely to put themselves out there.

Gottman broke down bids for connection into three types. The first is *turning toward* someone's bid. This is obviously the most positive response.

- A wife gets home from work, and her husband asks her how her day was. This is a bid for connection. The wife sits down and says that she had a really stressful day. They talk for a little while longer, and the husband offers to make dinner that night. The wife smiles and gives her husband a big hug.

- When a teenage son does his chores that his dad asked him to do plus an extra chore, this is a bid for connection. Dad sees the extra chore completed and gives his son a high five. Later that day, Dad takes his son out to shoot hoops.

In each of these examples, something happens that certainly doesn't happen in the next two types of responses to bids. What is it? It is the principle of reciprocity. Psychologists have found that when you make a prosocial gesture to someone, such as getting the door, smiling and saying hello, going out of your way to be helpful, people tend to respond in kind ways. That is to say, you get out of something what you put in. Kind of a like a relational version of Karma. "What goes around, comes around." If you put out kindness, you're likely to get kindness in return. If you put out respect, you're more likely to get respect in return.

The second type of response to a bid for connection is *turning against*. This is the situation in which someone makes a bid for connection, and the other person responds with hostility. Let's look at this type through the two examples mentioned earlier.

- A wife comes home, her husband asks how her day was, and she explodes on him for not giving her space.
- The teenage son does his chores and one extra. Dad sees the chores and scolds his son for doing them improperly.

This kind of response really does damage. Gottman has found that this response style ends relationships quickly. Why is this? Making a bid for connection is a vulnerable thing to do. The bidder is allowing himself or herself to be wounded in order to connect with the other person. So the other person's response matters. Think of it like a knight taking off his armor. An attack when the knight's armor is off does far more damage than when it is on.

The third type of response to a bid for connection is *turning away*. In this category, when someone makes a bid for connection, the other person's response is distance. Let's look at this type through the two examples mentioned earlier.

- A wife comes home from work, her husband asks her how her day was, and she doesn't even look at him. She walks upstairs to her bedroom and lies down. Her husband follows her up and asks again how she is doing. She turns the TV on and ignores him.

- The teenage son does the chore his dad asked him to do plus an extra one. Dad sees the chores and makes no comment. He doesn't praise or thank his son.

This kind of response can also be a relationship killer. People can often feel unappreciated, unmotivated, and lonely. This is the experience that the psychologist Sue Johnson describes as silent desperation. It also describes Sandra and Adam's relationship. In the next section, I will show how I helped them recognize their response type and what they could do to change.

Love, A Basic Human Need

Love is a basic human need. It's right up there with shelter, food, and safety. Love is not a luxury, it's a necessity. Therefore, to take a basic human need and make it conditional on good behavior is always wrong. *Love is not a bargaining chip when it comes to parenting.* Yet parents who fall into this thinking error often distort love in this way.

Imagine if a parent locked a child in the basement with no food until the child behaved correctly. Clearly this is wrong and punishable by law. But what is the difference between physical starvation and emotional starvation? I believe that in some cases, emotional starvation can be just as devastating, if not more so, to the well-being and development of a child. Basic needs should never be used as motivators for good behavior, especially love.

Furthermore, making the relationship conditional on good behavior tends to make the bad times very bad. In the case of Adam and Sandra, when Adam was in trouble, he was not only being punished for bad behavior, he was also being rejected by his mom.

Correction

Never make relational connection dependent on good behavior. That is not to say you do not have expectations of your child or do not discipline—quite the contrary. A loving parent-child relationship is based on expectation, instruction, accountability, and discipline. But expectation and discipline are not mutually exclusive to love and relational connection. I often tell parents I work with never to punish out of anger or desperation; *always punish out of love*. That last part may sound odd, but it is a key foundation for effective parenting. Sometimes, the most loving thing we can do as parents is to correct, reprove, and discipline our children.

Imagine if your child had an infected wound. The infection was life-threatening. The wound was itchy and prone to reinfection if exposed. The doctors gave you strict orders to keep your child from scratching. So, what do you do? The most loving thing you can do, of course. Every time your child goes to scratch or is scratching, you discipline, explain, punish, or offer an incentive. Whatever it takes, you do it.

Loving discipline includes two elements. First, which we have already discussed, have loving intentions as you

Making a bid for connection is a vulnerable thing to do. The bidder is allowing themselves to be wounded in order to connect with the other person.

discipline. In other words, the *why* behind your discipline. Second, *how* you discipline matters. Loving discipline involves providing a reason for the discipline. You must first have a set and understood standard for behavior in your family. When the child breaks the standard, consistently enforce the standard with corrective measures. If the child protests, asks why, or complains, gently but firmly explain your response (discipline) to the child's behavior. Consistency and remaining resolute are key.

Missed Opportunity

I once worked with a family where the young son had anger issues. Both parents loved their son, but had very different ways of responding to his rage. With the first parent, the son would rage at his parents inappropriately and unfairly. The parent would respond in kind and the conflict would escalate and reach a point of near violence. They would take a break, but then they tried to have a second discussion, the parent wanted to immediately talk about the problem. The son would get defensive and they were right back to the unproductive, escalated argument.

The second parent would respond to their son's rage very differently. She would let her son rage and then get distance that he needed. After some time passed, the son would return and want to do something with the parent that was unrelated to the argument like get a hug, go for a walk, play a game together. The parent allowed for this little time of reconnection and what she found was that after or even during a hug, walk or game, the child started addressing the problem in a calm, mature manner, which lead to a productive, honest conversation.

What the parents discovered, after the escalated argument, the child wanted some distance, but then returned to the parent to reconnect. Once the child felt reconnected and comforted by the parent, they felt safe to take responsibility for their poor behavior.

And when the second parent could follow this pattern, it turned a several hours fight into a 20-minute conversation that lead to healing and reconnection.

The first parent realized they were missing an amazing opportunity for honest, mature conversation with their child because they were unwilling to reconnect before addressing the problem.

Family Example

When I started working with Robert and Sandra's family, they were at the breaking point. They all felt that their needs weren't being met by the others. My biggest obstacle was getting Sandra to see the wreckage her shutting down and withdrawal of relational connection was causing. She struggled to see this because she was hyper-focused on the wrongdoing of Adam. Granted, she made good points. Adam was acting out, making poor choices, and disobeying. But this was no excuse to withdraw from Adam. Her shutting down was having unintended consequences she couldn't see.

Her shutting down blinded her to the positive bids for connection Adam was making. It's entirely appropriate to allow another person to reconnect and try to repair the damage when they know they've done wrong. Not allowing someone to do a repair is rather cruel. It shuts down the autocorrect process in relationships. Think about it. It's kind of scary putting yourself out there when you know you've messed up. Trying to repair damage you've caused is a vulnerable position to be in. So, getting your repair shut down hurts. Again, turning away from someone's repair attempts makes future repair attempts less likely. Sandra had to ask herself, why am I turning away from my son's repair attempt? Is it to add salt to the wound and punish him a little extra? Is it a power play? If I can reject his repair, I can hold something over him. Or were there positive reasons? Reconnecting without acknowledging the harm done—moving on without processing, in other words—isn't healthy either.

For Sandra, it was a combination of the three. She felt hurt, so she wanted to hurt Adam, and if she refused his reconnect/repair attempt, she had some power over him. And Adam was trying to reconnect/repair without repairing anything. He just wanted to move on and be back in the good graces of his mom without apologizing or acknowledging what he did. For Sandra, admitting what was really going on—her reasons for removing relational connection from Adam when he acted badly—was a big step. She felt prepared to make some changes.

From here I gave Sandra a set of very specific instructions to follow. When she was hurt, angry, frustrated, or disappointed with Adam I simply wanted her to acknowledge and recognize her feelings. These feelings were powerful forces that were driving her away from Adam when he needed her the most.

> *Most importantly, Adam felt Mom's love regardless of his behavior. This made it safe for him to admit when he acted badly.*

When Sandra learned to maintain her relational connection with Adam even when he misbehaved and let her down, her parenting became more productive. When Adam misbehaved, she had the skills to process what Adam did that wasn't right. This was a vastly better response than giving him the cold shoulder because this allowed Adam to process what he did and learn why it was wrong. That was the missing key and why Adam kept making the same mistakes over and over again. By shutting down and coldly distancing herself from Adam, Sandra wasn't enabling Adam to make progress. He was always stuck, and for that matter, so was Sandra. But when she kept the relational connection strong even when he did wrong, they were able to have great conversations. Mom could explain why Adam's behavior was wrong. They would sit and talk about things Adam could have done instead of acting on impulse. Mom then committed to praising and rewarding Adam every time he resisted an impulse and made an alternative/positive choice. And Mom was better able to give constructive feedback when Adam acted out because they had a mutual understanding of what was expected from Adam and how he could make efforts to improve. Adam liked this especially. Before, he was never sure of what he did wrong and why Mom was turning away from him. Now his mom wasn't turning away. She was giving feedback, and he was empowered to make wise choices.

Most importantly, Adam felt his mom's love regardless of his behavior. This made it safe for him to admit when he acted badly. He was no longer afraid of Mom finding out what he did and then feeling like she hated him. This was the most surprising result for Sandra. She always imagined that Adam would be more likely to not act out because he hated being shut out by her. This method had never panned out. But now that Adam knew Mom loved him regardless, he was less motivated to act out. He used skills to control his impulsivity and to admit when he acted out. He was more open to Mom's feedback and corrections.

Another way to describe maintaining relational connection regardless of your children's behavior is grace. Grace is a gift. It is not earned. When children have acted poorly, they have not earned your love. But when you give children grace, you allow them to learn, they feel safer coming to you when they have acted out, and most important, they are motivated to grow because of the relationship. Some of you might think, "But if I give my children too much grace, they'll walk all over me." Grace is not passivity. Grace addresses the problem behavior head on. Grace does not exclude discipline. Grace is the foundation for your parenting. It is what I discussed earlier: *loving discipline.* And—a nice little fringe benefit—it teaches children to be gracious. By your courageous act to be gracious in your parenting, you affect your children and their future kids and grandkids. You are leaving a remarkable legacy that will affect future generations when you parent with grace.

Chapter 7

I Will Respect My Child if My Child Respects Me

Hold yourself responsible for a higher standard…Never excuse yourself.
—Henry Ward Beecher[11]

Respect is a hard thing to give, especially when your spouse, friend, or child doesn't give it in return. It's even more difficult to give if your spouse, friend, or child is disrespectful. So, what do you do in response? Do you shut down? Do you get defensive? Are you saying things like, "I don't have to act respectfully because my child disrespects me", "I yell because they yelled first", or "I'll respect him once he starts respecting me."

Parents make the mistake of seeing themselves as morally superior to their kids.

If this is true of you, you are likely caught in a negative cycle that is very hard to break. The negative cycle has two characteristics, it is: self-

11. Joseph Demakis, *The Ultimate Book of Quotations* (Kindle Edition, 2014), 274.

perpetuating and self-reinforcing. The negative cycle is *self-perpetuating* because each person refuses to budge or change until the other person makes changes. If each person is unwilling to change until the other moves first, you have a stalemate. You are stuck!

It is also *self-reinforcing* in that a parent or child may assume the other is going to be disrespectful, so they act as if they are being disrespected, which then influences the other to then be disrespectful. Psychologists call this a *Self-Fulfilling Prophecy* (e.g. the assumption of disrespect creates the disrespect). So then, when disrespect does happen, it confirms the parent or child's assumption, and they feel vindicated in their negative perception of the other person.

This leads to many bad outcomes in the parent-child relationship.

Their Bad Behavior Justifies My Bad Behavior

When giving your child an instruction, have you ever had to repeat yourself over and over again? Have you ever felt like a broken record? This can be frustrating and stressful. None of us would admit this, but when our children act in such a way, yelling feels really good. It gets the tension out. Maybe all the pressures with work, spouse, and family has been building up, and so when our child acts out, that is the straw that breaks the camel's back. All of the tension is poured out. It's cathartic.

The bad behavior from a child gives parents license to yell, curse, and disrespect the child. Parents anticipate their child's bad behavior, using it as permission to yell, scream, and act poorly. Over time, this can create a toxic environment in your home.

John Gottman, a noteworthy psychologist and relationship researcher at the University of Washington, can predict with 94 percent accuracy if a couple will get divorced after a fifteen-minute meeting. He has discovered relational dynamics that are relationship killers. However, the most devastating dynamic is *contempt*. When one person sees themselves as morally superior, and the other as totally wrong, the relationship has little to no chance of being healthy or of surviving the long haul. Parents make the mistake of seeing themselves as morally superior to their kids. This creates resentment within our children, as it would with any other person, and ruins parent-child relationships.

We all know the immortal words of Jesus: "Turn the other cheek"[12] and the apostle Paul: "Fight evil with good".[13] In fact, most of us would consent that turning the other cheek is the morally right thing to do when wounded by another, but how many of us live this truth out? Nelson Mandela was unjustly imprisoned as a political prisoner. However, on attaining his freedom he did not seek to punish his captors. He forgave them and ended apartheid in South Africa. How was he able to break such a well-established and entrenched social evil? He fought evil with good. Since you are the parent, the burden of change is not on your child. The onus of change rests heavily on your shoulders. *If change is going to happen, it begins with you.*

Backfires

Have you ever found yourself explaining, "I tell my children all the time to respect me, but they never listen!" Some parents make the mistake of subconsciously thinking, "Do as I say, not as I do." However, this method always backfires.

Children respond to behavior.

Children follow parents' behavior.

Words reinforce actions, but they do not replace actions.

---

[12] Matthew 5:39, NIV
[13] Romans 12:21, NIV

Therefore, if the majority of your parenting is in *words*, and not in *actions*, children will surprise you by following the latter. In other words, if your words and actions are misaligned, you are setting yourself up for failure. As was said before, "Be the change you want to see in your children."

Demanding respect from your child without giving it also creates a power struggle. You are essentially overpowering or overwhelming the child's will with your own. Children internalize this as a methodology for problem solving. Lo and behold, they internalize your example and use it with others to disastrous results. Getting your way by imposing your will—a might-makes-right type of thinking—ruins relationships.

> *Whatever you want your child to learn, must be taught through the medium of your character and actions.*

Ask yourself: Do you want your child to be a bully? Do you want your child to get his or her way by overwhelming and overpowering others?

You probably do not want that for your child; however, by demanding respect without first giving it, you teach your child to overpower. If your child chooses to fight back, you end up with endless back-and-forth bickering. "You don't respect me, so I don't respect you." You both can make the same complaint of each other, and have the same reason not to change.

Being a parent doesn't give you a pass on respecting your child. Whatever you want your child to learn must be taught through the medium of your character and actions. Incongruence between your demands and behavior causes your child to lose respect for you.

This is different from the behavior of respectfulness. When you act incongruent, loss of respect becomes the perception. Giving respect ought to be a reflection of who you are. It is far easier for children to act respectfully when they respect the person in front of them.

Take an honest look at your parenting. Ask for feedback from friends, your spouse, even your children, and ask if this is true of you.

Correction

The most effective way to change a negative pattern isn't so much about stopping it as it is replacing it. What do I mean by that? If you put all your attention and energy into stopping the problem pattern, you won't be very successful. You must counteract the negative pattern by *replacing* it with a positive one. That means you must lead the way by showing respect, even when your child's behavior makes you want to be disrespectful. Leading with respect won't give you instant results. In fact, it's a hard road to travel, but it will give long-term results.

So, how do you lead with respect? When respect is modeled, it becomes *internalized* and then *externalized*. Let's break down that statement. Modeling is a basic psychological principle of learning, especially when it comes to kids. Children are innate observers. Watching, listening, and mimicking are powerful forces in shaping their behavior. So, when they see you being disrespectful, they learn disrespect. When they see you being respectful, that positively influences them. Certainly, there are exceptions to this rule, but generally the principle holds true.

What do I mean by internalized? Internalization is the process by which a child's behavior is influenced by what they see. Has your child ever seen a car drive by and then yell, "Brrrmmm" every time he sees a car thereafter? Has your child ever heard a dog bark and then pretend to be a dog by barking? This is the process of internalization. Children are exposed to a lot of things, but not every single thing they see becomes internalized. Externalization is the product of internalization. A child sees the dog barking and then externalizes that experience by barking herself. Furthermore, children are more likely to do what they see repeatedly.

So, your child sees you being disrespectful, using curse words, arguing versus discussing, belittling, demeaning, shouting, complaining, and so on. And what happens? They act out those disrespectful behaviors themselves. But remember what I said about repetition? This is another psychological concept called reinforcement. The basic idea is that whatever garners your attention and reaction is then more likely to happen again. Let's say every time your child complains when asked to do a chore, you respond by yelling. That behavior is more likely to happen again.

The good news is that these principles work both ways. You can model positive, respectful behavior that can be internalized and then externalized by your child. Also, you can make that positive respectful behavior more likely to happen consistently by reinforcement. It's a pattern that reinforces itself—a positive feedback loop.

So, what's the takeaway lesson? *You, the parent, must model the behavior you want to see from your child.* This requires a change in your thinking. Instead of focusing on what your child is doing wrong, look at what changes you need to make first. With time and consistency, your child will follow your lead and you will have a respectful relationship.

Furthermore, you are going to have to build distress tolerance for disrespectful behavior. That means you need to learn coping strategies to deal with disrespectful behavior from your child. Remember, when children are acting out, being disobedient and disrespectful, that's when they need you the most. That's when they need you to model respectful behavior the most. When you model respectful behavior when your child does not deserve it, it establishes a strong precedent. Over time your child will respect your character. You are a person who does not allow the bad behavior of another person to break down your standards of behavior. This speaks to the legacy you leave to future generations. If you can model respectful behavior in the face of disrespect, and your child learns from you and passes that along; what a powerful legacy you have left for posterity. Generations of your offspring to come will be leaders and models in their families and communities because you did something hard for the benefit of your child.

> *She would mock him for not going to school or getting a job. She called him a freeloader and a thug and say he was just like his father.*

Family Example

I worked with a single mom, Lupita, and her son, Carlos. Mom got pregnant in her teen years. She raised Carlos on her own as a teenager. Carlos has never met his dad. Mom suspected he was in prison (since he was in and out of prison when she knew him). Things were very difficult for them. Lupita had to work several jobs, and Carlos was often alone. He never felt like he belonged or was in a "real" family. He also missed the father he never knew.

As Carlos became a young man, he was drawn to the streets and other young men. He quickly discovered a whole new life outside his home. It was a life of violence, fear, and crime. But in the chaos of the streets, he also found a home in a gang. The gang was composed of other young men his age who also came from broken homes.

They provided one another with what they did not receive at home—a feeling of belonging. They looked out for one another, often supporting, protecting, and fighting for one another at the expense of their own safety and well-being. In the gang, Carlos found other young men who offered him a father figure, brothers, and friends. In the gang, he felt respected. Contrast those benefits with what he received at home. His mom was constantly tired (from working several jobs), distracted by tending to Carlos's brothers and sisters (Mom had children with other men after Carlos), or angry that Carlos was out with the gang. She didn't like the fact that he was in a gang doing criminal activity. She would lose her temper and curse and yell at Carlos. She would nag him about doing his chores, watching his siblings, and being out too late. She would mock him for not going to school or getting a job. She called him a freeloader and a thug and say he was just like his father.

Carlos had little tolerance for his mom. He was a young man who valued respect. His world outside his home operated under the single imperative of respect. If anyone violated this one code, they were punished severely. It took a lot of self-restraint for Carlos to not attack his mother. Although Lupita and Carlos had gotten into yelling matches before, and the police were called, it had never turned physical.

When I started working with the family, they recently had had a loud physical altercation. The police were called. As I spoke with the mom and son I realized their biggest complaint about each other was disrespect. Carlos complained that Mom disrespected him, and Lupita complained that Carlos disrespected her. They both wanted the same thing from each other but were unwilling to give it. Their retort to me when discussing respect was "I give [her or him] respect when [he or she] gives me respect." They were locked in this unchanging pattern of wanting respect, not getting respect, and not giving respect.

My message to them was very clear and brief. "If you want respect, you have to give respect." Short and sweet, right? Clear, straightforward, and easy to do, right? Wrong! You see, they both agreed with my message in principle, but in practice, it was another story. It was the hardest challenge for them to give respect. Why? First, giving respect required each of them to be vulnerable. This was something neither one of them was comfortable doing. Second, the moment either one of them slipped back into old habits, it threw the whole thing off. Third, all the past examples of the other person's mistakes and disrespectful behavior were present in their minds. When one did something that annoyed the other, past mistakes and bad behavior were used as ammunition.

However, it was immensely helpful to identify all the ways in which their efforts to create respect in their relationship would get off track. I think I had them work simply on identifying the triggers that would initiate the cycle of disrespect. Doing this helped for a few reasons. One, it made the problem the pattern that the two got stuck in. The problem wasn't Lupita or Carlos individually, but their pattern. Second, the more awareness they had about their triggers, the more control they could have over them. When you are aware of what you are doing, you can make choices. If you aren't aware, then you are acting reactively, without much control. Once they were competent at identifying their triggers, I initiated the second phase of my master plan.

Once they developed self-awareness, which gave them the opportunity to make choices, I had them work on what kinds of choices they wanted to make. They could choose to act in a way that was consistent with their values, or with the kinds of behavior they wanted to see from the other person. Not easy choices to make, but they started making choices to respect the other person. And wouldn't you know it, the more consistently they acted respectfully, the more the other person was likely to reciprocate. By acting respectfully, they launched a counter cycle of respect. Respect begat respect. Once they felt like their respect was received and returned, the more likely they were to continue the positive pattern. The police weren't being called, fights were quieter and more manageable, and still no one was using physical violence to resolve the argument. I think that's a win-win.

The idea of reciprocation is a carry-over from the last chapter. It is the idea that you get out what you put in. For Carlos and Lupita, they were too afraid to unleash the power of reciprocation. But with a few shaky steps, when they acted the way they wanted to be treated, it unlocked a positive pattern.

Chapter 8

Because I Said So!

Being powerful is like being a lady. If you have to tell people you
are, you aren't.
—Margaret Thatcher[14]

What do you think and feel when your son or daughter talks back or challenges you? What is your typical response? Have you ever declared those immortal words when challenged "Because I said so!" Interestingly, this declaration never inspires the reaction we're looking for in our children. Instead of stopping themselves short, reflecting, and obeying immediately, they tend to do the opposite. Children become more defiant and obstinate. Why does this happen? Why does the "because I said so" tactic never work?

Humans, regardless of who you are, tend to *fight fire with fire*. If your child is defiant, there is an impulse to meet that defiance with more defiance. Sir Isaac Newton, the eighteenth century British physicist, wrote "For every action, there is an equal and opposite reaction." This was his third law of thermodynamics and provides a key insight into parents with defiant kids. When your child is obstinate, *you* feel the urge to be obstinate. You match his obstinate behavior with your own, which, surprise surprise, lead to escalation.

---

14. Joseph Demakis, *The Ultimate Book of Quotations* (Kindle Edition, 2014), 423.

This pattern is like what you see on schoolyard. A bully will target the kid he's most likely to get a reaction from. If the bully can get under someone's skin, he's won. Now I'm not saying your child is a schoolyard bully. But there is something beneficial to notice about the process of bullying. Bullying feeds on itself. The more a bully gets a rise out of his target, the more power he possesses.

As a parent, you must be leery of getting caught in this pattern. And trust me—the pattern is insidious, seductive, and powerful. It will suck you in before you ever notice.

Being reactive is understandable, no one wants to be bossed around. In other words, no one wants to be lorded over. This idea is as old as the New Testament. In 1 Peter 5:3, the apostle Peter gave instructions to the leaders of the new Jesus movement, also known as the Church. He instructed the leaders to not "lord" their power over their flock or congregation, but instead, he encouraged them "to be examples." There's a lesson here for parents. Your kids won't respond to domination, or being lorded over. But they will respond when you lead by example.

> *Your kids won't respond to domination, or being lorded over. But they will respond to you leading by example.*

Lead by Example

If you don't like it when your child responds to a request with a groan, ask yourself whether you groan and complain when asked to do something. If you don't like it when your child shouts when angry, ask yourself if you raise your voice when you're upset. If you don't like when your child doesn't pick up after themselves, ask yourself if you pick up after yourself. Why? The quickest way to lose respect is to try to enforce a rule you don't follow yourself.

When you can demonstrate respectful, kind and patient behavior, even when your child is behaving poorly, that creates influence and authority. A true leader, like a true parent, leads by inspiring people on the basis of their character.

Clearly there are some qualifications to this. You must dominate your child with your authority in cases of their safety. When my daughter is playing with the power socket, I pull her away immediately and then put in a plastic socket plug, much to her dismay. I do this unilaterally without a discussion. However, as my daughter grows older, if I'm still using the same parenting approach as I did the with power socket, when it comes to negotiable things, I will lose her respect.

There are different *privileges* between adults and children, but the *standards* should remain the same. For example, as an adult you are privileged to drive a car. It's not a right. You must earn that privilege by passing a driver's test, paying for the car, paying for car insurance, and consistently driving safely. Your child does not have the same privilege.

But, when it comes to standards of behavior, the expectations should be the same. Just as you expect your child to be polite, so should you. Just as you expect your child to be respectful, so should you. It's not unfair that you have different privileges than your child. But it is unfair when you hold them to a different standard than you hold to yourself. When parents don't abide by this kind of thinking, it encourages kids to rebel.

Backfires

Parents who dominate their children usually feel as if they don't owe their kids an explanation for their expectations. They think, "Since I'm the parent, then I shouldn't have to explain myself. My child should just obey because they are the child." Here's a hypothetical situation which illustrates the thinking error. Let's say your child requests spend time with friends after school instead of coming home and doing chores immediately. And you ask them to provide an explanation for that request. You want to know why they want that, you are interested to hear their reasoning. Seems fair. Most parents do this. So, when the shoe is on the other foot, and you come to your child with an *expectation*, and they ask you to provide an *explanation*, is it fair to then get upset and say it's not your child's place to ask such questions? Isn't that unfair?

This is "Rules without explanation" parenting. When children are subjected to harsh expectations without a rationale, even when the expectations are in their best interest, they rebel.

You can look throughout the course of human history and see this same pattern playing out over time. Harsh expectations given without clear explanations usually end in revolt. This principle effects nations, states, cities, towns and yes, even the parent-child relationship. Your kids may not be taking up arms against you, but they are slowly building up their resistance toward your authority. You are losing relational ground every day you parent like this.

> *When you approach your child with a harsh startup, it won't end well.*

The Harsh Startup

One surefire way to know if you parent like this is if you are guilty of using the, what John Gottman calls, "harsh startup." Gottman found that couples who approach their spouse (when needing to have a difficult conversation, to correct the other person, or to give them feedback) in a harsh manner, the conversation is likely to end in a nasty fight. The same applies to you when talking to your child. When you approach your child with a harsh startup, it won't end well. Why is that? When an approach is harsh, it almost always raises the other person's defenses. I like to use the analogy of a castle surrounded by a moat that can only be crossed by a drawbridge. Open communication is like a castle with a lowered drawbridge. You can send your message to the other person (like peasants walking over the bridge into the castle) without trouble. But when you approach your child with a harsh startup, it's like the castle knows it's under attack and raises the drawbridge. All the defenses are raised, and nothing is getting through to the castle, including your initial point. At that point, the power battle will be won by whoever can shout the loudest.

That's the ironic thing about the harsh startup that many parents don't get. The point you initially wanted to get across gets lost in the defensiveness. Once that drawbridge is raised, your message isn't getting through. And sadly, this is a very sticky negative communication cycle. It can echo through generation to generation.

A Legacy of Dominance

Parenting through dominance establishes a precedent for your kids' future parenting and relationships. Every time there's a conflict between you and your kids, if the resolution is you shouting, "Because I said so" or some variation of this, you are teaching your kids to solve conflict through force. You are teaching your kids relational violence.

Imagine your daughter in ten or fifteen years working her first important job. She went to school, trained, and certified in her dream career. Yet, there's one problem, she can't get along with her boss. One day, the tensions come to a head. The boss doesn't like how your daughter handled a work-related issue. Your daughter, instead of discussing the issue, taking feedback, sharing her side of the story, chooses to yell. She mocks, belittles, and threatens her boss into submission. Why did she do this? Well, that's how she saw you handle conflict. The handwriting is on the wall. Your daughter loses her job and narrowly avoids police charges from her boss. The word gets passed around that your daughter is a hothead, a problem employee, and her career suffers for it.

Let's play out another scenario. What if she uses dominance in her personal relationships? Her partner puts up with for awhile, but over time, the resentment builds and the relationship dissolves. Sadly, this happens all the time. I have worked with clients, men in particular, who use physical and verbal aggression to control their partners. The reason they do this? Because they saw their parents do it that way. Using dominance, aggression, and verbal and physical violence to resolve issues leads to domestic violence and abuse.

A Legacy of Submission

The other side of aggression is submission. Your daughter, instead of solving all her conflicts through dominance, solves all conflicts through passive submission. In essence, your voice was so powerful it silenced your daughter's. Let's replay the work scenario over again, but with submission. Your daughter gets her dream job. She calls you overflowing with excitement that she got the job. Yet, over time you notice her joy diminish. You ask if anything is wrong. She doesn't respond. You ask again. She says nothing until the silence is broken with her tears. She admits to you that her boss has been making sexually aggressive advances. You are enraged and ask why she hasn't done anything about this. Your daughter in a hushed tone says there was another girl who was fired because she shot the boss down. She's afraid to lose her dream job or for another girl to be the target of the boss's attention. So, she suffers in silence, passively accepting what's happening at work. She's afraid to stand up for herself because she learned that conflict doesn't lead to solutions.

Conflict only leads to more pain. She learned that from you and this is the consequence.

The last backfire to parenting by dominance is that it encourages your son or daughter to follow without thinking. Think about it. "Do what I said because I said so!" doesn't allow your child to internalize your reasoning. You used logic and values to arrive at your rules. But your child doesn't understand the reasoning behind the rule; all they see is the rule. I think it is a greater gift to your children to teach them to think rather than to just obey. Children who obey because they see the logic behind your rules will obey you consistently and without much resistance. Children who obey because they are afraid of you or feel forced will obey inconsistently and with resistance.

> *The basis for authority is not grounded in title or position. It is earned.*

Furthermore, teaching your kids to think by the vehicle of explaining your rules is one of the greatest gifts you can give them. More often than not, kids have little by way of critical thinking skills. A price tag cannot be put on teaching your child to think critically.

Correction

How do you correct this dangerous thinking trap? You must understand that authority is earned, regardless of position. To use another work example, we've all had that boss who is a pain in the neck, who has a lot of demands, but offers little help. The kind of boss who has high expectations of respect, even though he or she does nothing to deserve the respect. This kind of leadership fundamentally fails its employees. Why? The basis for authority is not grounded in title or position. It is earned. A boss who earns their title creates relational capital with their employees.

Let me ask you this: If no one likes that kind of boss, why do you think it's OK to be that kind of parent?

If you don't want to be that kind of parent, you must ask yourself how do I earn authority? First, change the way you think. Change the expectations you have of your kids. They shouldn't follow or obey purely because you're their dad or mom. They are motivated to follow and obey because you are a person of character, consistency, and servant leadership. Here are five ways to achieve this goal:

Rules with Reasons: This was explained in detail in the last chapter, but it's worth revisiting in this context. Thinking you don't have to explain your rules to your child is a mistake. Taking the time to explain your rules shows that you respect and care for your child. It also increases your child's "buy-in." That is a term which means your child's level of investment in the rules. If they are invested, they are more likely to consistently follow them. If they are not invested, then they likely won't consistently follow them.

Humility: Be humble enough to adapt rules when your child raises good criticism. Don't be afraid of listening to your child's feedback regarding your rules or even your parenting. When your child has a voice and input regarding the rules they are expected to follow, this again increases their "buy-in." It also increases respect. Just like at work, employees respect a boss they can be honest with— in parenting, kids respect a parent they can be honest with.

Negotiations: Do not fear negotiating. It increases "buy-in" from the child. When your child offers a sincere objection to your rules do not dismiss them or get defensive. Rather, be open to their suggestions and use the opportunity to engage in negotiation. Based on your child's feedback, you may end up with a negotiated set of expectations that is far better than the previous set. Give your child the benefit of the doubt unless they've given you reason to doubt them.

Servant Leadership: One of the most effective forms of leadership that has been observed throughout human history is that of the servant-leader. Servant-leaders garner respect by being honest and caring, working hard, sticking to their word, and above all, leading through service to others. Lead your kids by example. Model the kind of behavior you want to see in them.

Soft Startup: The soft startup is the antidote to the harsh startup, as if that weren't obvious already. The soft startup is all about your *approach*. Think again of our castle with the moat and drawbridge analogy. If the castle sees an invading army (a harsh startup) it will raise its defenses and drawbridge. But if the castle sees an ally approaching, it will keep its defenses down and the drawbridge open.

So, what is the soft-startup approach in practical terms? It is a strength-based, understanding, solution-oriented, skill-based approach that says, "I'm coming as your ally." If you approach your child in an attempt to understand what happened, it will ease your child's defenses. If you look for what the child did right just as much as for what went wrong, it will change the dynamic for the better. If you approach your child looking for a solution (What skill needs to be developed? What choices were made? How can we do better next time?) answering these questions will help your child grow. If you approach your child with the idea that their mistake was due to a lack of skill and not defiance, they will be more open to you. Now imagine if you combined all aspects of the soft-startup approach into one seamless encounter with your child. Would it help? Would it allow you to make a change in your perspective? When you are not on the warpath but coming as an ally, do you think it would help your child be more open to what you have to say?[15]

---

[15] Aspects of what was described above are part of a new approach to oppositional

Influence: I think parents who get caught up in the because-I-said-so style of thinking genuinely want to influence their children for the positive. The only problem is, you can't influence someone whose defenses are raised. Influence is a soft skill, not hard one. If you try to ram influence down your child's throat, it won't be digested. If your child's drawbridge is down, you can send your influence into the castle. I think this is generally true for most people, including you. No one likes being forced to change, but everyone is open to influence for their benefit. You have years of wisdom and experience, but it matters little to your child if you are forcing them to change. Allow your child to benefit from all that you have to offer by giving what you have in a winsome way.

One Final Caveat

What I have described above is about laying a firm foundation. Yet, if you are in a situation where you have not laid that foundation, and you are now trying to follow these suggestions, but your child isn't helping you— and by not helping you out I mean they are challenging your rules, even when you give an explanation— I suggest limiting how many times you explain yourself. If your child truly wants to engage in a thoughtful, meaningful conversation about the rules and your reasoning, then by all means, have that conversation. But, if your child is questioning your rules as a manipulative tactic to push your buttons, then stop explaining your rules and simply enforce them. This will require you to be to be discerning when your child is being sincere or not. There are many ways in which you can discern when your child is not being sincere, yet one way I've observed when working with families is when the

---

children called Collaborative and Proactive Solutions (CPS) developed by psychologist Dr. Ross Greene. The approach assumes children struggle because of a lack of skill, not a willful disobedience. For more on this approach, I recommend reading Greene's *The Explosive Child*, and *Lost at School*.

child will question the rules after they've violated them. What I've suggested is that parents share that they are open to their child's feedback, but that conversation is to be had when everything is calm, there's no conflict, and the child approaches the parent with legitimate concerns. However, when the child has *violated the rules*, that is not a time to have a meaningful conversation *about the rules*. It is likely the child is only saying what they are saying because they don't like being in trouble. So, *make Monday's conflict, Tuesday's conversation.*

Family Example

These corrections remind of me of the time I worked with an older couple, Candace and John, and their oldest son, James. Candace and John were "old school." They valued respect and being respected. They were raised in an era when you respected your elders, followed authority figures, and didn't question the prevailing wisdom the time. They thought it wasn't a child's place to question, but to obey. So, when their son James back-talked, questioned, or didn't respect them, they came down on him hard. Things would escalate, and James would scream, "Why should I do what you say?" John and Candace, almost in perfect unison, would retort, "Because I said so!"

Early on, John and Candace were able to assert their will strongly enough to keep James in line. But as James grew, he became more willful, stubborn, and unwilling to follow Mom and Dad's direction. Their fights would get so bad John and James would get into physical fights. James felt isolated in the home and oppressed by his parents. He ran away for weeks at a time and used drugs and alcohol when he was missing. He drank to the point of harming himself. On several occasions, James drank so much he was hospitalized. This only made John and Candace redouble their efforts. The few times James was home, he had all privileges restricted. He was to go to school and couldn't see his friends. If he broke or questioned the rules, all his mistakes were thrown in his face.

Around this time, I started therapy with the family. The family felt like they were at an all-time low. James was out of control, and John and Candace were scared. James would say things like his parents didn't care for him. They just wanted him to do what they said. The parents told me that ever since James was a little boy, he was always defiant. As I learned the family's story and each person's perspective, I quickly discovered that John and Candace were both deeply invested in James. In fact, they loved him and cared about his well-being, and they couldn't understand why James was so reactive. They thought he must have some kind of disorder. I shared with them that whether he had a disorder or not, the changes in their parenting would be the same. For example, if James had reactive attachment disorder or he was just out of control because he was making bad choices, the advice I would give them would be the same. This surprised them. So, what advice did I have for them? I said I thought it was their intent to influence James in a positive way. They didn't just want him to do the right thing; they wanted him to have the skills in order to make the right choice on his own. At this point, Mom and Dad nodded in agreement. If that was the case, when they used the because-I-said-so approach every time they encountered resistance from James, they were sabotaging their efforts to influence him. In other words, that approach raised James's defenses like a drawbridge. At that point, it didn't matter if they had the most profound, beautiful, life-altering piece of wisdom to share with James, his drawbridge was raised.

> *But even their failed attempts worked with James because he could see that they were trying.*

They asked me, "What should we do?"

I said, "Change your approach."

I slowly walked them through each correction bullet point as described above. I said that they needed to explain the reasons for their expectations. Be humble, work toward negotiating with James to create buy-in, be servant-leaders, and use soft-startup skills, and he would open himself to their positive influence.

I'm sure you know that unlearning a long-held habit takes time, and it did for this family. Mom and Dad had many lapses in their attempts to try the new approaches I recommended. But even their failed attempts worked with James because he could see they were trying. Once he saw his parents really working hard and trying to create a better relationship with him, he upped his game too. His running away became less frequent, he reduced his intake of drugs and alcohol, and he agreed to attend a GED class two days per week. I wish I could say I miraculously fixed all the family's problems, but this kind of progress was exhilarating for the family. Any movement in the right direction was a win. And more important, they had momentum that empowered them to keep tackling the issues in their family.

In cases like Candace and John, the answer isn't to change the parents in order to change the family. Nor is it if you change the child, you change the family. Change must be a group effort. What do you do if you want change, but your kids don't? Parents can be agents of change. An agent of change is different than an enforcer of change. Parents can influence their family to work together by changing themselves first, in the way they respond to their family's negative behavioral patterns. When you change your approach and the way you respond to your kids, that influences them in a positive direction.

Chapter 9

That's Not How You Were Raised!

Children are educated by what the grown-up is and not by his talk.
—Carl Jung[16]

Y ou'd be surprised how many times I've heard parents in my counseling office say to their kids "You weren't raised that way." The phrase is usually uttered amid some kind of chaos. Either the child has done something wrong or the parents have reached their stress limit. When I ask parents about the irritating behavior from their child they usually give me a story about how their kid got caught up in the wrong crowd at school. "It's their fault!" But as I work with these families, I tend to make the same observation over and over again. *The parents act out, without any self-awareness, what they punish their children for.*

The crux of this thinking error is that some parents believe there is a difference between what they *say* and what they *do*. In principle, these parents tell their children to be respectful, pick up after themselves, don't drink alcohol, and obey the law, generally good parental advice. But in practice, these parents break every rule. So, what do kids learn from them most? As I've discussed in previous

16. Joseph Demakis, *The Ultimate Book of Quotations* (Kindle Edition, 2014), 380.

chapters, children are keen observers. They learn from what they see, not from what they are told.

Another way of putting it, these parents are essentially operating from a "Do as I say, not as I do" mentality. They think, "It doesn't matter what I do as long as I tell them the right thing to do." This leads to a confusing and disorienting contradiction in the child's life. They are to listen to their parents and ignore their actions. This causes children to lose respect for their parents. Why? Children learn more from their parents' behavior than their lecturing, so of course they mimic parent's bad behavior.

This problem seems so obvious, why can't parents readily see the mistakes they are making? Why are parents so blind to the apparent contradiction between what they do and what they expect from their kids? I think the answer is twofold.

The first reason is genuine blindness. Not literal blindness, but the lack of self-awareness—*a blindness of character*. For whatever reason, parents who hold this thinking error assume they are immune from behavioral influence. What does that mean? It's simple: what you say and what you do *both* influence your kids. Here's how I break down influence from parents:

Verbal influence (what you say): minimal influence

Behavioral influence (what you do): major influence

Congruent influence (what you say and do): maximal influence

Incongruent influence (contradiction in what you say and do): negative influence

I will say more on each of these bullet points later, but for now note that incongruence isn't ideal.

The second reason parents are blind to this thinking error has to do with fear. They are afraid to admit that their behavior is immature. They are afraid that once they face their true selves, they will be forced to change. There is no doubt these are difficult things to confront. It makes sense that some parents would push uncomfortable truths away— ignorance is bliss. Yet, it is those blaring blind spots in our thinking, behavior and character that cause parents the most harm. Our blind spots create repeated backfires unless we face and deal with them.

> *Words affirm your actions. Words do not replace actions.*

This may be hard to admit, but ask yourself if this manner of thinking is true of your parenting.

Backfires

The shocking truth (which really isn't shocking at all) is that children model their behavior after their parents' behavior. If a parent says one thing and then does another, children will follow suit. Your children will do as you do. And they'll usually act out what they see at the most inconvenient times, at moments of greatest embarrassment.

There are no passes when you are a parent. Everything you do is observed and noted by your child. Not on a conscious level, but what you do is more important than what you say.

Words affirm your actions.

Words do not replace actions.

Think about the sources of parental influence listed in the last section. Verbal influence is minimal compared to behavioral influence. If you see a division between your verbal influence and your behavioral influence, you're in trouble. The two should not be separate. The incongruence erodes your authority, influence and level of respect.

Subtle Harm

I once knew a young man whose father was a gregarious, outgoing, and beloved member of his community. However, in several key areas of the father's life, his words didn't match his actions. On the surface, the father seemed like a wonderful dad. But no one could see the hidden cracks in the foundation. Over time, the young man grew to respect his father less and less. The young man eventually left home and refused all contact with his family and his father. The father was congruent in serious moral and legal areas, but he was incongruent regarding his beliefs and actions. This was confusing for the son and it was enough to subtly harm their relationship.

Credibility

You may or may not be thinking that incongruence is a problem, but not a serious problem. Certainly, not an issue that warrants a whole chapter in a book. Yet, based on my clinical experience, I've seen incongruence compromise a parent's credibility, time and time again. When asked to stop a behavior that their parents do, a child can say, "But you do it too." Kids are keenly aware of the fairness or lack of fairness in the structure of how the family and home are run. If they have demands put on them by someone whom they don't respect, it will backfire time and time again.

This thinking error may lead to the greatest loss in parent's opportunity for positive influence. We too often take the negative perspective in many aspects of our culture. Our medical system focuses on disease diagnosis and treatment instead of preventive care. We focus on the unemployment rate instead of areas of economic growth. We focus on sensational crimes in the media instead of the global decreases in murder, warfare, and terrorism. Culturally, we love to watch the train wreck. This also carries over into parenting. When your words and actions are incongruent, it not only negatively affects your child, you lose your platform for positive influence. Incongruence is like stuffing your child's ears with cotton balls. When you have something beneficial for them to hear, the message isn't received.

Correction

If it the statement "That's not how you were raised" has little impact on changing your child's behavior, why even make the statement? The statement is meant to shame our kids. The statement also misplaces blame. Parents who are guilty of thinking error place blame on anyone other than themselves. They will complain about their kid's friends, the TV shows they watch, or the sports figures they love. That isn't to say friends, TV and sports heroes don't have an influence on our kids. What influences our child isn't as simple "how they were raised." There are many *layers* to influence.

To understand the forces that influence our kids it's important to know the work of Uri Bronfenbrenner. Bronfenbrenner was a developmental psychologist who postulated an *ecological theory* of child development. Bronfenbrenner says there are four major systems that influence children: microsystem, mesosystem, exosystem, and macrosystem.

The **microsystem** is the immediate environment in which the child plays, lives, and learns. Included in this system are family, friends, and organizations like school, church, and other community groups. It could be nurturing or hostile, which could either empower or inhibit the child.

The next system, the **mesosystem**, describes how different parts of the microsystem relate to one another for the benefit or detriment of the child. An example of this kind of relationship is a dad coaching his daughter's middle school soccer team or a mom participating in the parent-teacher association (PTA). And the quality of those relationships matters too. If the dad is a lazy coach, that negatively affects the child. If the mom is a proactive and helpful participant in the PTA, that positively affects the child.

The third system is the **exosystem**. This system includes people, groups, and places that may not have direct contact with the child, but still play a major role: the parent's workplace, the kind of neighborhood the family lives in. If the workplace relocates the family, it has a massive impact on the child. If the child's neighborhood has high levels of crime, that has a powerful impact on the child.

Last is the **macrosystem**. This system is the largest in scale, the most removed from the child, but it still plays an influential role. People, groups, and places included in this system would be the government, personal rights, the cultural milieu, the relative health or decline of the economy, and so on. When the economy takes a dive, that impacts the child's state or city, which could impact their quality of living. If a child lives in a war-torn country, that could affect their access to healthcare, education and physical safety.

When you are congruent, you are happier. When you are congruent, you are a better parent. So be congruent!

There are many systems that influence a child. How a child was raised is one factor, maybe the most important, in what influences a child's development. Effective parents consider every layer of influence that is interacting with their child. They don't assume that their voice is the only voice. Therefore, effective parents take great effort to know their child's friends and their friend's parent's. They are involved in their child's education and extra-curricular activities. They know what their kids watch on TV or online. They research the games their kids play and are careful with their kid's social media use. "That's not how you were raised" thinking gives words undue significance. Unfortunately, the world we live in doesn't afford a simplistic view. Our kids are being influences by many sources, and effective parents understand that. Effective parents know it's their words being congruent with their behavior that matters. AND, their level of understanding and involvement with the outside sources of influence that matters.

Selective Responsibility

Why is it that parents are comfortable taking credit when their child does well, but when their child acts poorly or makes an unwise choice, the parent had no part to play? This simply cannot be true. This is taking selective responsibility and effective parents don't do this.

Parents need to be courageous and take responsibility for how they influence their children. Now, that isn't to say parents need to take credit for *everything* children do. Children are responsible for their actions. But parents can take responsibility for how they influenced their child in addition to genes, environment, culture, personal psychology, family of origin, religious training or lack of it, and so on. There's a lot to consider.

Effective parents make sure their words match their actions. What you tell your children will take on significance when bolstered by your actions. Be congruent, which means there is an agreement between your beliefs and actions. When you are congruent, you are happier. When you are congruent, you are a better parent.

This is a point that Brené Brown makes in her book *Daring Greatly.* She makes the point that who you are is more influential than what you say. Your character, personality, and lifestyle are more influential than how you raise your child (in the narrow sense as defined above).

If you are a person of integrity, that is the greatest influencer you can give your child to be a person of integrity. This is true because your actions are an outflow of your character. Jesus once said, "The good person out of the good treasure of his heart produces good, and the evil person out of his evil treasure produces evil, for out of the abundance of the heart his mouth speaks."[17] The context for this bit of wisdom was the analogy of a tree. If the tree was good, it produced good fruits. If the tree was bad, it produced bad fruit. That is to say, who you are determines how you behave and what kind of influence you have on your children, *not* how many times you said something.

Family Example

I once worked with a family who struggled with this thinking error. Mom, Marian, and her son, Douglas, were responsible for the brunt of the fighting. Dad, Drew, worked long hours, so he was rarely home. Marian and Douglas fit typical patterns that are true of most relationships. They had very similar temperaments. Mom recalled that she struggled with many of the same things that Douglas struggled with at school. They both had a hard time connecting with others of the same gender. In addition, they had a hard time paying attention in class. They both had low grades and behavioral issues with school authority. You'd think all the similarities would foster mutual understanding and connection, but this wasn't so. The similarities made their conflict worse.

---

17. Luke 6:45, NIV.

Add to the equation other stressors like low-income, rough neighborhood, and a little support from extended family. That meant Mom was on her own with six kids most of the time. This kind of situation either brings the best out in parents or the worst. Mom, because she was often tired, overwhelmed, or irritated, relied more on her words than her actions.

Furthermore, the house had little structure. It was ruled by her will, which was determined by her mood and energy level. She often said, "That's not how you were raised" when frustrated with Douglas. She would ask him to do a chore, and he would say he would do it later and then not do it at all. He would go to a friend's house and not return for hours without checking in. Sometimes he would leave without asking permission. The icing on the cake for Mom was the time when Douglas got into a physical fight on the school bus. Another boy was mocking Douglas, and he hit him. Mom was furious when she heard about the fight.

Douglas and mom thought the same way, argued the same way, and pushed each other's buttons in the same way. They would have no-holds-barred fights. They would scream, yell, and ridicule. Neighbors would hear them yelling and call the police. It was a regular occurrence to see a police car parked in front of the house.

Drew, when home, was able to play the part of the peacemaker. He could separate the two of them and then talk each one down. He was especially effective in speaking to his son. He could help his son process his feelings and think through situation. With his wife, he could be a sounding board. He would listen and validate. However, when he pointed out that they were similar, they both thought he was crazy.

Dad's statement about their similarity made Douglas furious. He refused to see himself being in any way similar to his mom. He had no respect for her. Mom insisted that Douglas lacked regard for women in general. Yet Douglas often told me that girls were the only kids he got along with at school. The boys made fun of him and didn't include him during recess. He often got into fights with other boys (the school bus, for example) and said being around the girls calmed him down. His biggest complaint was that his mom was a hypocrite. He said she was furious with him about the fight on the school bus, but she would hit him often when he was younger. He said she pushed and derided him over homework, but he knew that she got poor grades and never did her homework when she was his age.

> *Many of the things she hammered Douglas on were things she currently did, or previously struggled with.*

When I started working with the family, I pointed out almost immediately what Drew had been saying for years: Mom and son were similar. That similarity got them into a lot of trouble. It added fuel to the fire. I also observed that Mom had utterly no awareness that she raised her child to be just like her. Everything her son learned, he learned from watching his mom. And this was the source of their conflict. All of her words (verbal influence) were invalidated by her previous and current actions (behavioral influence). When she demanded that Douglas do his homework, her words had little power. She expected him to respect her, but Douglas thought of all the times she mocked, derided, or belittled him, so he mocked, derided, and belittled her. When she reprimanded him for fighting at school, he thought of the all times she slapped him across the face when he wasn't listening.

Over the course of counseling, there were some fireworks between Mom and myself. She did not like what I had to say. At first, she refused to see Douglas' behavior as a reflection of her own. Fortunately, I had Drew there for the first couple of sessions. There were several points at which Mom left the room and Drew calmed her down. However, once the sting wore off, Mom was able to accept my observation and begin taking responsibility for her contribution to the problem. This was not a "Douglas" problem, although I later clarified that Douglas was responsible for his own actions as well. This was a relationship problem, one in which Mom needed to stop focusing on what she *said*, and look at what she *did*. Many of the things she hammered Douglas on were things she currently did or previously struggled with.

Mom admitted that when she saw Douglas's bad behavior, it made her feel ashamed. She felt guilty that she let him down and that she couldn't parent him more effectively. She also felt ashamed of her own behavior as a child.

Douglas's behavior was a constant reminder of that shame and embarrassment. But she didn't have skills to parent Douglas, so she repeated with her kids what she learned from her parents. However, once she was able to admit the way Douglas acted was in fact the way he was raised, Douglas softened up. He respected her for taking some responsibility. I can't say that their relationship was fixed after that, although they did begin communicating with each other. Fights became strongly worded conversations instead of escalated conflicts. Douglas checked in with Mom before he left for a friend's house, and at school he used some skills we discussed in counseling to handle conflict with other boys.

These small victories were a big deal to a family that only knew losses. The gains this family made you can have too. I can't predict what kind of victories your family will have, but I can say with confidence that only good things can come from correcting this thinking error and replacing it with a better way of thinking. When you become more congruent, your influence has a greater, more positive   impact.

Chapter 10

I'm Afraid to Discipline

The child supplies the power, but the parents have to do the steering.
—Benjamin Spock[18]

Have you ever felt afraid to discipline your child? If you answered "yes" to this question, do you know why? Some parents fear that if they discipline their child, their child won't like them anymore. These parents put their personal needs for approval above the developmental needs of their children. Parents do this is because they wrongly seek approval and affirmation from their children. This is a dangerous thing to do for many reasons. Kids are not meant to bear the emotional needs of an adult.

Some parents are also concerned that if they discipline their child, that will inhibit their learning. These parents think their child will become so afraid, angry, or hurt that they'll miss the point. These parents err on the side of caution to a fault. There's nothing wrong with being careful in how you address your child, but caution, in this case, is likely more about protecting your feelings rather than providing *discipline* for your child. Discipline enables children to learn from their mistakes. It provides them with

---

18. Joseph Demakis, *The Ultimate Book of Quotations* (Kindle Edition, 2014), 383.

boundaries and feedback. Without boundaries and feedback, children will remain developmentally stuck.

A big reason often given by parents who avoid discipline is that they don't want to damage their kid's self-esteem. This is where self-esteem becomes a shackle as opposed to a tool. As we will discuss later in this chapter, a key aspect of discipline is *feedback*.

Feedback offers your child the opportunity to grow and progress, which leads to living an empowered life. If you remove discipline from the equation for fear of hurting their self-esteem, you are effectively removing the possibility of personal growth as well. This is a terrible handicap to give your child. As does every parent, you want to give your child the best you can. Shirking discipline is not giving your child the best. I would argue for replacing self-esteem altogether with another term that starts with "self." I believe in the power of *self-efficacy*.

Self-efficacy is the belief that an individual can accomplish what they put their mind to. It is the belief that they are a capable person that is resilient and can overcome obstacles via their own skills, support from their community or through trial and error (i.e., learning). This, speaking personally, is a vastly superior way of thinking about oneself than self-esteem.

Avoiding discipline comes with tradeoffs. Parents who get nervous when it comes to disciplining often prefer being their children's friend. If this is you, remember that it's a preference that comes with a price. If you settle in as your children's friend, you will lose authority and respect. Your children may like you, but they will not follow you, respect you, or respond to your persuasive appeals. More importantly, avoiding discipline and being your child's friend is a poor motivator. Kids don't feel indebted to their parents when they don't discipline, they feel entitled.

Many parents are shocked that being their kid's friend didn't work. This type of thinking backfires for parents and can have repercussions for into adulthood. I've worked with several parents who have adult children still dependent on them for basic life needs.

Backfires

Parents who avoid discipline put their personal feelings above the needs of their children. Children need discipline, structure, and accountability. But if you are paralyzed by your personal need to be liked, you are doing your children a disservice. The absence of structure is unstable for children. They have developmental needs for discipline, structure, accountability, instruction, consistency, and parental expectations.

> *Parents who err on the side of friendship compromise their own authority.*

Parents who err on the side of *friendship* compromise their own authority. Children won't respect parents who shirk their role and want to be their friend. Sadly, I've worked with this issue many, many times. This has already been discussed at length in chapter 2, but it's important to reiterate it in this context. What eventually happens when it comes to discipline issues is the parent who prefers the friend role resorts to *bribery*. How does this work? Well, it works (and backfires) in two ways.

Rewards without Effort

Parents who are friends won't discipline, so in order to get their children to do something like chores, go to bed, and give respect, they give in to their children's demands and wants. This may work in the beginning, but it only has temporary effects. The child will take and take, knowing that there are no consequences. And once a child starts to push boundaries and encounters no push-back, will continue to push the limits of what they can get away with.

I remember a family I worked with where the parents were terrified of imposing structure and discipline. Things got so bad, the child was arrested and put in detention. When the child was released back into the home, the first thing the parent did was to get the child a new smartphone. The child was overjoyed, but after a few days, the honeymoon period wore off and the child was back to their old behavior. The parent was at a loss. They couldn't believe why their child was behaving so poorly. They said to me "I gave them a new phone and they are still acting like this?!"

I told the parent that they were rewarding their child in the hopes that they would feel grateful and then behave well. This is wrongheaded thinking. I then said, *you should only reward a child when they've done something to earn the reward.* Don't reward them hoping it will inspire good behavior, because, I can assure you, it won't.

I shared with them that children, in general, are motivated *earning a reward, avoiding a consequence, achieving a goal,* or having something social scientists call *relational motivation.*[19] Motivation is not engendered when the reward is given out of the gate— it negates the reason to work and try hard. It also creates an expectation of what will happen in the future. More on this in the next section.

Bad Behavior without Consequences

Children learn quickly how the situation can be taken advantage in two ways. They know that they get a reward after doing something wrong as illustrated in the story just shared. They also know parents give in to their demands if they push their buttons. If they hold out

---

[19] This is motivation generated to achieve a goal created by the quality of the relationship between parent and child.

long enough and cry loud enough, their parents will give them what they want. This tactic works because kids know that friend parents have a low threshold for their temper tantrum behavior. Parents who want to be friends are easily swayed by their children's manipulation.

I hope I don't sound like some bitter, kid-hating, children-are-the-spawn-of-Satan kind of person. I've just seen, what I described above, happen enough times to know it happens. It's not meant to be a slam on kids. It is just an accurate descriptor of adolescent behavior. Trust me, children are smart. If they can work a situation to their advantage, they will. In fact, we all do this. It's just that kids get caught more often because they are more obvious about it. This is the human condition, and we shouldn't be blind to it.

> *It isn't appropriate to depend on your child's emotional approval and support for your own wellbeing. That does not provide a stable foundation for a child.*

Correction

If you need *emotional approval* and support from your child, you will be putty in their hands. You need to find another source, outside your children to meet your emotional needs. That should be a need satisfied by a friend, partner, spouse, community, faith, family member, or mentor, but not by your child. Now, that isn't to say you cannot have a close bond with your child. It is appropriate to be vulnerable with your child. Parent child relationships are emotionally rich relationships.

But *a parent shouldn't be emotionally dependent on their children.* That does not provide a stable foundation for a child.

Discipline and Boundaries

Discipline also provides opportunities for your child to learn *boundaries.* Discipline is kind of like spell check on your word processor. You hit that button and you have instant feedback on where your document is off. Your computer will also show you where your text isn't within the margins, or where your grammar is wrong, or where your formatting isn't right. This is incredibly helpful since can go back through and correct your mistakes. Discipline functions in much the same way. Discipline lets you know where you went wrong and what you can do to fix it. There have been many times when I've crossed a boundary and didn't know it until after the fact, when my wife or a friend told me I went too far. This was invaluable information that allowed me to either make an apology if needed or be more mindful in the future. Without that discipline, I would have kept making the same error. It works the same for parents. When you discipline your children, you set them up for success because they won't keep making the same mistake, or they will make the mistake less. They will know what is acceptable and unacceptable behavior. But, in order to communicate effectively with your child where there are and are not boundaries requires giving feedback.

Discipline and Feedback

Discipline helps your child learn how to take and process *feedback* in a way that benefits them and their relationships. Feedback is to life as water is to a thirsty man…or something like that. OK, maybe I didn't say that right, but feedback is really, really important. Think about it for a moment. What if you lived in a world where there was no feedback? You would never know when you damaged a relationship. You would never know why you failed your driving test. You would never know why you had to pay so much in taxes. Basically, this is a world that doesn't work. Feedback is essential for progress. You can't grow without feedback, even when it's hard to hear. Your kids will not progress if you don't give them feedback. Feedback is a tremendous gift you can give your children.

Also, receiving feedback in a healthy and gracious manner has a positive effect on relationships. If your child puts himself out there and offers you feedback, he's intentionally putting himself in a vulnerable position for your sake. Giving feedback takes guts. It's not an easy thing to do. Therefore, if you take to heart what he has to say, it shows that you care. If you thank him for sharing his thoughts, it makes him feel respected. You can even disagree, but as long as you are processing the feedback in a manner respectful to your child. It's not easy, but if you can follow this advice, you will help the relationship.

Ideally, seeing the benefit of teaching children boundaries and the ability to receive feedback through discipline empowers you and them. Discipline helps your children grow and progress. Your son can feel emboldened because he knows, deep down he's capable of learning. He doesn't have to be stuck, wondering why he's stuck. He can elicit feedback from friends, coworkers, and family for his betterment. It doesn't have to be a scary thing because you demonstrated discipline in a healthy way. If that doesn't fire you up, then I don't know what will.

Discipline Plan

Discipline does not need to be a confusing and complicated process. The more clear and straightforward it is, the better it will go. Discipline usually involves a predetermined plan that includes your child's input. I walk families through the plan-making process in 4 steps:

Step 1: Start with a list of *expectations*. Begin with a general outline of what you want from your kids and then get more specific. For example, you want your children to be respectful. What does that mean? Be specific. Respect is your child making eye contact and giving you undivided attention instead of looking at a phone or TV.

List out each expectation and then define it. I would then recommend going over basic things like curfew, chores, friends, and weekends. I love it when I turn to kids and ask them what their expectations are of parents. They look flabbergasted and delighted. Expectations should not be for parents only. Kids should have a say in what they want from their parents. And every time I've asked kids what they expect from Mom and Dad, I've gotten sensible, surprisingly mature responses. They too need to list their expectations and then define them.

Step 2: Discussing expectations usually involves some *negotiation*. This it totally appropriate. I've noticed when parents and kids negotiate their expectations and come to an agreement, maybe not total agreement, there is more buy-in on both sides. So, be willing to compromise. You may not get all that you want, but if you engage in negotiation, you are more likely to get some of what you want as opposed to nothing.

Step 3: Determine what *consistency* is. This is a vital part of the plan. It's so important because I've seen families get bogged down in the I-did-the-chore, no-you-didn't fight. Sadly, I have been witness to parents and their kids fighting about who did what and when, too many times. Kids often claim they met their parents' expectations, and parents claim they didn't. Why does this happen? It happens because consistency hasn't been defined in a measurable way. Think of consistency as the unspoken expectation on the list of expectations. Don't just tell your kids what you want them to do, but how often and to what extent. That means making it clear that you want the bathroom cleaned three times a week. I also suggest getting some kind of whiteboard so that you can track when the chore or expectation is due or completed.

Step 4: Establish *consequences* and *rewards*. Again, I recommend allowing your kids (if they are the appropriate age) to participate. When children can offer ideas for their own consequence or reward, they are more likely to follow through. The nice thing about establishing consequences and rewards beforehand is that you can be consistent. Consistency on your part is just as important as consistency on your child's part. You need to be consistent in giving rewards and consequences when you said you would. Not giving rewards when you agreed to give them only kills motivation. Not giving consequences when you agreed to give them costs you respect. So be consistent.

Discipline and Self-Efficacy

Discipline helps children learn *self-efficacy* because discipline supplies the structure in which children can succeed. If your children make a mistake, you provide them with feedback from which to learn and improve. In doing so, children learn that they can conquer what they struggle with. They are not powerless in their situation. They are not powerless in what is difficult.

Albert Bandura wrote in his classic textbook *Social Foundations of Thought and Action: A Social-Cognitive Theory*, "People who regard themselves as highly efficacious act, think, and feel differently from those who perceive themselves as inefficacious. They produce their own future, rather than simply foretell it."[20] Discipline creates an environment where your child can become "highly efficacious." This is one of the greatest gifts you can give

---

20. Albert Bandura, *Social Foundations of Thought and Action: A Social-Cognitive Theory* (1985), p. 395.

your child. Helping children become highly efficacious gives them the tools to "produce their own future."

Too often children accept the world around them as a given. The world is what it is, and you can't change it. But is that true?

Are we to simply accept our lot in life?

Is that the kind of mentality you want your child to possess?

What if your child lands a dead-end job?

Or is in an abusive relationship?

Even worse, lives in a totalitarian country where the government is abusive?

Wouldn't you want your child to feel empowered to change their life or the conditions around them?

Frankly, self-esteem can't deliver this kind of empowerment, but I think self-efficacy can. The part you play is to foster self-efficacy in your child. And the seedbed for self-efficacy is a disciplined environment in which your child can learn, grow, and overcome obstacles.

Family Example

I worked with a family that was really struggling with discipline, structure, and feedback. The dad, Jerome, had recently married a woman named Vanessa. Things were good at first, but eventually Vanessa had problems with Jerome's oldest son, Jalen. The problems started when Vanessa observed Jerome being lenient with his son. Wanting to help and contribute to the family, she tried compensating for Dad's leniency with structure, a lot of structure. As you can imagine, Jalen didn't love the changes Vanessa was making. Jalen complained and Jerome took it up with his new wife. Again, this did not go so well. Vanessa thought her husband was taking Jalen's side. The house became a war zone with clearly divided allegiances.

When I started working with the family, I asked Jerome about discipline. He said he was always nervous when it came to discipline because he felt guilty over his divorce. He felt like he damaged his child and he had to make up for it. He also stated that he and Jerome were best friends. On the one hand, I could relate to Jerome. Divorce is a painful thing. It destroys the foundation of a child's life, the family unit. However, being overly lenient, being a friend, and avoiding discipline didn't help. In fact, it made things worse.

Think about it this way. If a child was struggling because life was unpredictable and unstable, why would you remove something predictable, stable, and consistent like discipline? I asked the dad this, and he saw the logic in what I said. I added that Jalen needed a dad more than ever. His parents' relationship was lost; he didn't need to lose his dad too. Jalen has and will have many friends, but he only has one dad. Dads provide love and discipline (as do moms).

Unpacking this for Jerome helped him realize that the real reason he avoided discipline wasn't because his son was hurting and needed slack, it was because he needed love. Losing his relationship with his wife because of the divorce left a hole in his life. He was lonely, and he needed connection. He sought connection from his son. He wanted his son's love and approval. Therefore, he was very lax with the rules, gave in to Jalen's demands, and indulged his son's requests for video games, having friends over, and skipping school. When Vanessa came along, she challenged and disrupted this pattern. Jerome didn't see his mistake and took his anger out on her. However, once he could see the pattern, Jerome was able to patch things up with Vanessa and reestablish discipline, structure, and feedback with Jalen.

Jerome was losing his son, but discipline restored their relationship. If you find yourself dependent on your child, feeling guilt and wanting their approval, or uncomfortable with authority, take a page out of Jerome's playbook and start with the basic. Start with the expectations exercise. Use that as a platform to start providing your child with firm, consistent and loving discipline.

Chapter 11

What Worked Before Will Work Now

What got you here won't get you there.

—Marshall Goldsmith

"What got us here won't get us there" is a rather famous axiom in the business world. The idea is simple enough. What worked to get your initial success won't work in the long run. The fact of the matter is that companies have to keep evolving in order to continue growing. In the business world, success can lead to stagnation which can lead to death. But how can that be? How could success ever be equated with death?

The reason being, success makes companies comfortable. They go on cruise control. Success makes companies lose their "edge." In other words, they stop innovating, adapting and learning. And the same principle applies to parents.

Parents make the mistake of thinking, "I can use the same parenting strategy that worked when my child was at a younger stage for my child who is at a later stage of development." It makes sense, right? If you stumble upon something that yields positive results, then you keep using it. That's just common sense. Unfortunately, this is where common sense fails you.

The parenting strategy that worked before may not work in the future. You must keep adapting to the developmental needs of your child. And I get it—that's a hard thing to do. It's hard to remain in a state of flux. Humans are creatures of habit. We like to settle into a pattern and never change. And unfortunately, it leads to bad outcomes for parents.

When you find something that works with your kids, it's like a comfort zone that you don't want to leave. The downside of staying in that comfort zone is that you don't progress as your kids develop. Eventually, your kids will outgrow your knowledge of what works. This will present you with a choice: do I learn from this situation and try new things? or, stick to what I know and refuse to change?

Rapid change is happening at a rapid pace, although it may not feel like that all the time. Sometimes parenting can feel like the days are long and the years are short. This puts great demands on the parent to face discomfort, learn from experience, find a pattern, and then experience discomfort again. Constant back and forth between not knowing and mastery. And some parents aren't up for all the work this requires. They settle into one pattern and then never change. It doesn't matter if that one pattern worked or not. Sticking with one pattern denies the need to change and adapt as your child develops. This kind of thinking can be catastrophic for parents.

Backfires

Adaptation is the name of the game. By not adapting, you create conflict. The reason being, before you know it, your children are ready for more. They are ready for more responsibility, for more feedback, for more freedom, and if you refuse to match that readiness, you hurt your child's development. It causes pain, and they will lash out as a result. Or, their development will be stunted.

Inobservant

To add fuel to the fire, your child's needs and changes invisible. Wouldn't it be so much easier if your child woke up one morning and announced they would like more autonomy? Unfortunately, kids don't do that. Therefore, it's important to *observe* the changes in your child's thinking and behavior.

I spoke with a parent who told me that the day her daughter turned fourteen she was like a totally new kid. Suddenly, she was really into high heels, makeup, and wearing dresses. As a side note, I had to compliment this mom because paying attention to children's preferences can give an insight into their thinking, into their inner world.

Yes, change and development really can happen that fast. The opposite is also true. Your child can develop in such a way that you don't even notice. You aren't even aware that they changed in an important way.

> *Adaptation is the name of the game. By not adapting, you create conflict.*

Overly-Observant

The other danger is to over-adapt. You want to strike a balance between adaptation and consistency. If you are overly-observant, and therefore overly influenced by the changes your child is making, it could lead you astray. As kids grow older, their self-concept, preferences, and feelings change frequently. I'm sure parents of teenagers would argue they change on a daily basis. This observation actually has some truth to it. Psychologists and counselors are restricted from giving hard and fast diagnoses for clients who are minors (under eighteen) because a minor client could present one way one day and another way on a different day. This kind of turbulence is normal, and it's important not to get too carried away with it. No matter how old or young your child is, he or she will always need love, relational connection, structure, accountability, predictability, consequences, and reward.

I once worked with a family where the parents were good parents. They had effective strategies, and they were consistent and meant well. The only problem was their strategies were appropriate for a young adolescent and not for a teenager. These parents loved their son, but whenever he encountered a problem at school, with friends or personal ones, they would take over and come up with solutions for him. Being that hands-on was not an appropriate match to the developmental stage of their child. The son wanted to work through challenges on his own and then use Mom and Dad when he felt like he needed them. Something as simple as this led to big fights, the son running away, and the parents changing their attitude from one of caring to resentment. Such a simple parenting mistake had catastrophic results.

The simplicity of the problem made my work both easy and hard. It was hard to get the parents to see how what they were doing didn't work. But once they were persuaded, the changes they implemented were easy. They allowed their son to struggle and work through problems on his own, and they simply made themselves available to help, but not to take over. Adapting to their son's development stage meant changing their *roles*. They went from being hands-on to being hands-off in many regards. This was a tough transition at first, but after some time, they settled into the new role and enjoy grew to enjoy it.

Correction

The truth of the matter is that old strategies don't work with new stages of development. When I work with parents who struggle with this, I like to use an analogy to illustrate this point. When your child is younger, you play the role of a *benign dictator*, meaning that you have total control, but you're nice about it. Your control is intended for your child's best interest. You can tell your daughter to eat her vegetables, when to go to bed, when to brush her teeth, and so on. And if she doesn't want to do it, you can control that too. You can put her to bed early, give a time-out, or even go old school and put her in the corner. Regardless of what you do, you call the shots.

However, I wouldn't suggest doing this with a teenager or even an adolescent. Why? Because those strategies are no longer effective based on the developmental stage of your child.

Back to the analogy. When your child is older, your role changes to that of the *president* of a democracy. In other words, your control now rests in relationship and influence. So when it comes to something like bedtime, that's an expectation that can be negotiated. Your child can have input on when it is. I even suggest that parents allow their kids to barter if they are willing to follow a condition. For example, "I'll allow you to stay up thirty more minutes if you do the dishes and take out the garbage tomorrow." Just make sure they follow through with the condition. If they don't follow through, then I wouldn't barter with them until they can demonstrate follow through.

Buy-In

Establish rewards and consequences for consistency with chores and following house rules. I often coach parents and their kids through this process. The best part though, is when teenagers realize that their opinion matters. So, when they offer a suggestion or a change in expectations in order to earn a reward they really want, they are more motivated to follow the rules. I call this the *buy-in*. Buy-in is when a teen takes ownership for involvement in the home and family. These teens are invested because they are working for something they want or care about. I've seen this especially when it comes to sports. I have seen teens who struggle with academics work extremely hard so that they qualify to play a sport they enjoy.

Incentives

Don't ignore the power of incentives. I've seen parents resent their children because they only get motivated to follow a rule or do a chore because there is something in it for them. Well, let me ask you: Would you go to work if you didn't get paid? Would you spend time with someone whose company you didn't enjoy? Would you go to a movie if you didn't want to see it? The fact of the matter is that humans are universally motivated by reward and incentive. Don't resent your children because it is also true for them. Instead, use the universal principle to your advantage.

> *At the risk of sounding repetitive I say again, match your parenting strategy with your child's stage of development.*

Relational Motivation

Regarding the relationship piece in the president of the democracy analogy, as I've discussed in previous chapters, your child will give respect when you balance expectations and demands with *relational connection*. I know I'm sounding like a broken record, but I can't say this enough. If you only have demands, your child will resent you. If you have no demands, your child won't respect you. Social scientists have found in study after study that the optimal parenting style is one that balances the two: parental demands and expectations combined with relational connection.

My analogy of the benign dictator and the president of a democracy are limited. There are other roles, analogies, or illustrations that can be used, but the point remains, match your parenting strategy with your child's stage of development.

Family Example

Gary was a great dad. He had a precocious and adorable nine-year-old son. He worked hard at a lucrative job, participated in the PTA, attended synagogue, and really cared about the foster-care children in his community. Gary cared so much that he decided to become a foster parent. He didn't allow a busy schedule with a lot of demands at work and being a single parent discourage him from taking on a foster-care child into his home. He applied and was approved within a week to take in a young man named Branden. Branden was sixteen and came from a bad home life. His biological dad was a drug addict. Growing up, he was often left unsupervised for days on end. Brenden was several grades behind, and in the few years that preceded moving in with Gary, he had bounced around from family member to family member or friend.

When Branden first moved in, everything was great. Gary and Branden got along. Their personalities complemented each other. Branden enjoyed Gary's nine-year-old son. He even started a GED program and looked for a job. Things were going well until they had their first fight. As you can imagine, given Branden's history, simple things like structure, accountability, and keeping a schedule were difficult for him. He wasn't used to these things. He wasn't used to having to ask for permission to leave the house to see friends. He wasn't used to a curfew. He wasn't used to Gary giving him restrictions when he got in trouble at his GED class. Gary wasn't doing anything out of the ordinary; he was just implementing positive changes. Sadly, Branden's struggling caused conflict between him and Gary.

The reason they got into so much conflict was that Gary expected Branden to be developmentally where he was chronologically. In other words, Gary assumed that Branden had the skills and maturity that any other sixteen-year-old would have. Even though Branden was sixteen years old, because of his upbringing he lacked critical skills. Even worse, he didn't know how to handle conflict. Every time Gary approached him about an issue, he reacted with hostility. As time went on, things got worse between them. Gary couldn't understand the developmental needs of Branden.

I started working with this family when things were at a crisis point. After a lot of conversation and validation, I was able to make some key observations. I suggested to Gary that his foster parenting was geared for someone developmentally sixteen years old. He agreed. I then made the point that although Branden was chronologically sixteen years old, he wasn't developmentally sixteen years old. Gary needed to view Branden's struggles from a skill-building approach. Up until this point, Gary saw Branden's behavior as laziness or rebelliousness. Developmentally speaking, Branden was not at the *adolescence* stage, he was still in the *industry versus inferiority* stage.[21]

In this stage, kids learn how structure works and what is expected of them. They learn how to personally meet the demands of their structure. For example, at this stage children might be given a weekly allowance. If they want to buy a big-ticket item like a new bike, they will need to save up their allowance. However, if they blow their allowance every week and then complain they don't have enough to buy the bike, the correct parenting choice is not to give in to the complaint. The child chose not to save their money. They,

---

[21] See the psychosocial stages chart on page 149.

instead, gave into *instant gratification* desires like candy and cheap toys instead of choosing *delayed gratification* desires like saving for a bike.

Choices lead to consequences and that's an essential lesson kids need to learn. This is just one example. The same principle applies to things like bedtimes, having friends over, doing chores and homework, and checking in. This manner of thinking applies to many different problems and if the child can adopt this way of thinking, it will benefit them for the rest of their lives.

This information reframed the problem for Gary. He could see that even though Branden was a teenager, because of the trauma from his past, he hadn't reached the developmental milestones of his peers. Gary felt compassion and empathy for Branden. When Branden made simple mistakes, or didn't think his actions through, instead of getting fired up, Gary responded calmly. He discussed with Branden where he made a mistake and what he could do differently next time. When Gary could see Branden respond to this approach, he felt encouraged that he was parenting Branden effectively.

Change, adaptation, and being flexible are not easy things to manage as a parent. We juggle so many balls at once, the necessity of adapting to our child's ever-changing developmental needs can feel like an assault to our sense of stability. Yet, effective parents aren't satisfied with staying in their comfort zone. Effective parents recognize the need to change how they think about this problem. They understand and accept the need to change and adapt as their child develops. But take courage, effective parents are not *born*, they are *made*.

If you're like Gary, take comfort in the fact that other parents struggle with this too. The greatest danger is not that you made a mistake in your parenting, but that you didn't learn from the mistake.

Chapter 12

My Parenting Style Is Just Fine

Imperfections are not inadequacies; they are reminders that we're all in this together.

—Brene Brown[22]

We all have a sense of style. We all dress in a particular way, listen to a certain type of music, read certain genres of books, and connect socially in our own way. Style is an expression of how we see ourselves. But style has a dark side. Unconsciously, we judge others based on our own standards. Do they match with our style of doing things or not? If they do, we like them. If they don't, we don't like them. There's nothing wrong with doing this per se. Where style becomes problematic is when we lack awareness. We simply judge others based on our individual style of doing things. In other words, we assume our style is absolute truth. Parents can be guilty of this problem too when it comes to their parenting.

Parents can falsely assume that their way of parenting their children is *the right way* to parent child. This is a serious thinking error and can limit parent's growth in 2 key backfires.

Backfires

---

[22] Brené Brown (2010). *The Gifts of Imperfection: Let Go of Who You Think You're Supposed to Be and Embrace Who You Are.* Simone and Shuster, p.76.

When we assume our style of parenting is the right style of parenting we limit ourselves in two key ways. First, the thinking error blinds you to the weaknesses of your parenting style. Second, the thinking error renders a parent unwilling to learn from the strengths of other styles. Let's examine these two limitations more closely.

First, *no parent is perfect*. No parent has the perfect strategy, style or method. It's just not possible. Therefore, I can say with confidence that every parent has something to learn. Every parent has an area of weakness. It should not damage your ego to admit this, yet, I've worked with many parents who do. It worries me greatly when I work with a family where the parent shares that they have nothing to work on, they are simply present for their child.

There are no two ways about it, if you think you have nothing to work on then you are effectively blind to your weaknesses. You are not dealing with reality. You are rejecting reality. And what happens to parents who think this way is that they live in denial. Their egos are too fragile to face their own limitations and weaknesses. And a parent who has a weak ego is not an effective parent.

Second, if you believe you have no weaknesses, then you are likely closed off to any feedback regarding your parenting. This leads to dangerous outcomes. *Relationships in general cannot function when feedback is restricted.* Marriages fail, communities collapse, businesses close, friendships implode and parent-child relationships are damaged when one person cannot share with their loved one, feedback. Feedback is essential to healthy relationships.

Correction

Effective parents identify what style of parent they are. This creates understanding about a parent's style and then allows the parent to hone their strengths and work on their weaknesses. What are the parenting styles I'm referring to? I'm glad you asked. There are four major parenting styles: authoritarian, authoritative, permissive, and neglectful. Depending on the type of parent you are, there will be costs and benefits. As you read about each one, think about which style best describes you. You may relate to one as aspect or another of each style. But you are looking for which style generally is the best description of your parenting.

The **authoritarian** style of parenting is a mix of high demands and low relational connection—the "Drill Sergeant" style of parenting. This kind of parent has all the power and is not open to negotiation. You can often hear this type of parent say "My word is law" "Because I said so" "Don't talk back to me." Their demands are high, their standards are strict, and the expectations rigid. They expect a lot out of their kids, but offer little in terms of support. These parents emphasize respect over and above friendship, which can hurt the relational connection between parent and child.

Strengths: High expectations are appropriate for parents to have of their kids. I am worried by the parents who have no or little expectations of their kids. Authoritarian parents provide their kids with structure which is helpful for child development.

Weaknesses: A strict environment with high expectations and little to no support can crush a child. An overly rigid structure can kill motivation, curiosity and create resentment. There is little affection and fun in these houses. This is not a balanced style of parenting. It takes the good of structure, discipline, parental demands and expectations to an extreme.

Outcomes: Children with this type of parent often rebel. This kind of parenting style inspires a *battle of wills*. The point of the relationship becomes who will win the power struggle. Kids purposely try to foil the parent. They make rash decisions to defy the parent. They feel as if they have no voice, so they use their behavior to speak. This entrenches the parent in their position even more. Often times, kids run away from the home or escape to the military.

Recommendations: Keep the structure, but make it more flexible. Praise your child's effort, not their achievements. Push your child to greatness, but give them support when they need it. A need for support is not a sign of weakness. Feedback is not disrespect. Prioritize your relationship with your child.

The **authoritative** style of parenting is a mix of high demands AND high relational connection. This is the "Servant-Leader" style of parenting. This kind of parent expects a lot from their kids all the while offering support and connection. This parent is willing to explain their expectations is open to input and negotiation. The servant-leader leads their kids by example, influence and relationship. But doesn't neglect the need for respect, structure and kids fulfilling their roles in the family.

Strengths: This style balances the need for expectations, structure and authority with support, flexibility and empowerment. Kids feel like they have a voice. This encourages child involvement and engagement in the rules, expectations and structure of the family.

Weaknesses: This style has been shown by many studies to be the most effective. I highly recommend learning this style and implementing it with your kids.

Outcomes: This, as attested by my experience and as the data shows from many social science studies, is the optimal parenting style. It balances parental authority and demands with relational needs and connection. This style enhances the bond between parent and child. It promotes love, care and responsibility. It best prepares kids for their future, giving them life skills in order to launch from home.

Recommendations: Balance expectations, standards and parental demands with support, guidance and understanding. This style encourages respect while maintaining a base of friendship. Parents address their kids with assertiveness, but they make room for their child's thoughts and opinions. When you practice this style of parenting you leave a positive legacy for your child that will benefit them in every sphere of life.

The **permissive** style of parenting is a mix of low demands and high relational connection. This is the kind of parent who wants to be their kid's "Friend." This parent wants to be liked by their kid. They have lax structure, loose expectations and flexible parental demands. They give provide their kids with a great deal of freedom. They deeply desire to have a great relationship with their kid and are willing to sacrifice anything in order to get that.

Strengths: Friendship, love, affection and fun are essential aspects of any good relationship, and that's true for parents and families. Kids feel understood, encouraged and supported when the relationship is safe. Children of these parents feel like they have a voice and can share what's going on with their parents. They know they can be who they really are with their parent.

Weaknesses: A lack of boundaries, structure, and expectations can be detrimental for child development. Children learn and are motivated by getting a reward, avoiding a consequence, or achieving a goal. Permissive parents don't provide this kind of environment, unfortunately. Permissive parents practice poor emotional boundaries with their kids. Children of permissive parents will struggle with self-discipline. They will struggle with accepting the consequences for their behavior. They will struggle with the word "no."

Outcomes: The outcomes of this style parenting is that parents sacrifice authority and respect in order to gain friendship, which makes the parent child relationship dysfunctional. These kids often walk all over their parents because they know they can get away with it. There are no consequences enforced for bad behavior. Kids are over-indulged and they aren't given life skills or a realistic picture of how the world works. And when it comes time to launch from the home, they are dependent on their parents. I've often worked with this kind of parent and they are flabbergasted as to how things got so bad. They're frustrated that their kids don't respect them and don't have any ambition for their future.

Recommendations: Establish and define your expectations and consistently enforce them. Be your child's parent, not their friend. That doesn't mean you can't be friendly, or enjoy aspects of friendship with them. But your child will have many friends throughout their lifetime, but only one or two parents. At the outset, your child will likely push back on these changes, but be firm. You will need to stand your ground when they challenge you. But firmness is the most loving thing you can do for them. Trust me, you don't want to be the parent seeking my help with their adult child who still lives at home.

The **neglectful** style of parenting is a mix of low demands and low relational connection. This is the "Absentee" style of parenting. This kind of parent simply isn't present, either physically or emotionally. This parent neglects their kids emotional, relational, physical, and developmental needs entirely. This happens because the parent works too much, or has an addiction, or is selfish. This parent provides little in terms of structure, discipline, consistency, rewards and consequences. They provide no relational or emotional support.

Strengths: Sometimes kids need distance. In fact, it is appropriate, to a degree, to let kids work through problems, conflict and struggles on their own. It can be unhealthy if a parent is overly involved. Many times, I've had to encourage parents to practice healthy, emotional detachment from their kids when they are too emotionally invested.

Weaknesses: Yet, on the other hand, too much distance can be a bad thing. Being emotionally and physically removed from your kids is irresponsible. Kids need to have their basic needs met by their parents. They ought to be supervised by safe people, in a safe environment. This is not what a neglectful parent does. The neglectful parents put their own needs, desires and wishes above the needs of their kids. Kids need engaged and involved parents.

Outcomes: It's no surprise that kids of this kind of parent are seriously unprepared for life. They run amok because they have no structure, no guidelines or guidance. These kids usually struggle with anxiety, have anxious or avoidant attachment styles (that means they have a hard time connecting with other people), and have little motivation to achieve a goal. The extreme cases I've worked with are very sad. Usually, a state agency is involved and kids get ripped away from their families and homes.

Recommendations: Get involved and engaged in the life of your child. Establish consistent and healthy habits of supervising your kids. Make sure their physical and emotional needs are being met. Prioritize their needs. It is healthy and appropriate to have expectations, structure, discipline and rules in your home.

Parenting with Style

I can't encourage you enough to follow the *authoritative parenting style*. It is far and above the best parenting style for kids and parents. I strive to practice this style of parenting with my two daughters. I'm not perfect, but when I aim for the right target and fall short, I come much closer to the goal.

It is your task to assess your parenting style. Like I said at the beginning of the chapter, likely you possess some traits from each style. But it helps when you can find the style, in general, that best describes you.

Then, have an honest conversation with yourself or with a trusted friend or fellow parent about your weaknesses. The absolute most dangerous choice you could make is to ignore your weaknesses. Living in denial only hurts you and your parenting. Admit to where you need to grow and start the hard work of change.

Challenge yourself with these targets—and if you fall short, at least you know you're going in the right direction:

- Expect a lot of your kids while supporting them.
- Sometimes relational needs will supersede your rules and expectations—be okay with that.
- Respect your kids—they will respect you in return.
- Focus on the positive steps your kids take—look for progress and not perfection.
- Be open to feedback and discussion—when your kids can voice their opinions, there is greater buy-in for the rules they have to follow.
- Don't over-emphasize your kids liking you. Being a good parent might jeopardize being "liked"—be okay with that.
- Encourage negotiation when your child disagrees with an expectation.
- Be willing to explain your rules and expectations.
- Be open to feedback and input from your child.
- Don't forget to have fun and enjoy your kids. They are imperfect and flawed just like you, so have grace.
- Earn your authority as opposed to assuming it.
- Lead by example.
- Balance authority with relationship by explaining rules and choices to your kids.

Chapter 13

Shaming Is My Best Parenting Tool

Shame, blame, disrespect, betrayal, and the withholding of affection damage the roots from which love grows. Love can only survive these injuries if they are acknowledged, healed and rare.

—Brene Brown[23]

P arents fool themselves into thinking shame is a necessary part of parenting. It is a thinking error to believe that shaming a child is effective and comes with no ramifications. This simply is not true.

Some parents associate shame with discipline, consequences, accountability, teaching personal responsibility, and correcting bad behavior. Yet, these objectives of parenting can be achieved without the harmful effects of shame. This raises the question, what is shaming?

Shaming a child is the attempt to correct behavior by publicly or privately humiliating or embarrassing them. It is to forcibly humble your child by pointing out what they did wrong and what that means in terms of their identity and character. For example, your child lied

---

[23] Brene Brown, *The Gifts of Imperfection*, p. 26.

because they are a liar; your child stole because they are a thief; your child used drugs because they are a drug addict. Guilt, on the other hand, is the response to doing something wrong and seeing the consequences it caused.

Shame is an ineffective discipline strategy at best. At worst, it causes developmental damage to your child, kills motivation, and hurts your relationship with them. This is not just a statement based on my personal perspective. Many mental health professionals in the field of psychology such as Brene Brown, Carol Dweck, Alan Kazdin agree that shaming a child only damages their development. Studies show that shame is ineffective at changing bad behavior and motivating good behavior. And, in my clinical experience, I've seen shaming backfire in the face of many parents who use it as a parenting strategy. Shaming creates power struggles between parents and kids. And I've consistently observed, over time, shame encourages kids to rebel. The parent who shames their kid loses respect. Shame results in kids feeling defeated.

But if shaming is all you know to do, and you take shaming away, what are you left with? Is there another way? Are there other tools parents can use to discipline their kids, keep them accountable, and give consequences for bad behavior? There are so many tools at your disposal that not only mitigate the damage done by shame, they are effective at motivating your child, fostering their development, enhancing self-efficacy, AND, most importantly, they build positive relationship between you and your child. So, what do you have to lose by giving up shame?

Backfires

The purpose behind most parent's actions is to influence their child in a positive way. Shame is influential, but in a way, you don't want it to be. Shaming your child poisons the well of their relationship. What does that mean?

Let's say you shame your child to discourage them from doing a bad behavior. Your child stops the bad behavior, but in the process of shaming them, you lose credibility and trust. Your child will not feel safe around you. I've worked with enough families to know that when kids don't respect or trust their parents, it puts a brick wall between the child and their parent.

Parents use shame as a way to correct a child's bad behavior and motivate them to do better. These are good goals. But how you achieve those goals— correction of bad behavior and motivation for good behavior— is just as important as what the goals are. And the how, shaming, doesn't work. Shaming is like using a flamethrower to start a campfire. Shame is an assault on your child's identity versus feedback on their behavior.

In my experience, parents shame their kids because they were shamed when growing up. And if you are doing something because that's the way it's always been done, how then do you know if it's effective? Maybe, it's time to reexamine shame as a tool for parents and to ask ourselves, are there better, more effective ways of parenting?

Correction

The positive intent behind shaming is a desire to influence our kids. Fortunately, there are many methods of influence that are effective and build relationship. Below I've listed several key ideas, but this is a short list. So, don't limit yourself to what is listed.

Rationale for Rules: If you can't give a reasonable explanation for your rules, then they probably aren't good rules, and they won't be followed by your kid. Have a calm, rational conversation with your child where you explain the reasoning for your rules. Let them ask questions. Kids are more likely to follow rules they understand and see the benefit of.

Honest Conversations: Have an honest conversation with your child regarding what they are *really* doing. If they are smoking weed, sneaking out to parties, hanging out with destructive peers, you need to know this so you can take appropriate action. The only way your child will tell you this information is if they feel safe. In order for them to feel safe, you can't freak out when they tell what's going on. Stay calm. Listen. Understand where they are coming from. Then offer guidance, feedback and instruction.

Understanding: You need to understand what your child thinks about the rules. You need to know why they won't follow them. Or, where they have an issue with the rules. Even if you don't agree with their perspective, at least you know what they're getting hung up on. This is valuable information. Often, parents think we know what our kids think, but we really don't. Once you understand, then you can discuss.

Positive Reinforcement: Rewards are motivators. They should always come with conditions. The logic is very simple "If you do X, then you get Y." This is not an ironclad rule, sometimes it can be flexed.

Do not put the cart before the horse. Meaning, do not reward your child hoping that will encourage good behavior. Rewards should follow good behavior. Don't bribe your kids, instead, motivate them.

Negative Reinforcement: Often kids understand your rules and the reasoning behind them. They question you because they just don't want to follow the rules. If this is the case, lead with enforcing the behavior you want. If they don't obey then remove privileges, freedoms and access to rewards. Again, *this is done for motivational purposes, not retributive.* If your child thinks you are being retributive, then they will fight back, resist, and challenge you at every step.

Buy-In and Relational Motivation: I know, I know, I've talked about these two concepts a lot, but there so good they're worth repeating. A positive relationship with your child can also be a motivator for them to follow the rules, understand your rationale, and be respectful. This requires you being respectful to them; to model the kind of behavior you want to see from them. The relationship is the most important thing you have with your child. Sometimes, you must put the relationship over and above getting what you want. If you have a good relationship with your child, meaning there is a positive connection, shared interest, good communication, respect, investment in each other, love and affection, your child will listen to you, follow your lead, and receive your input. They will have a high level of buy-in regarding the household structure and expectations.

> *Shame is ineffective, hurts your relationship, and demotivates kids.*

Don't make the mistake of being dependent on shaming. Shame is something everyone feels without it being intentionally added to our lives. Shame is ineffective, hurts your relationship, and demotivates kids. There is a plethora of tools available to parents that really work. So, do yourself and your child a favor and start learning how to use these parenting tools.

Family Example

Eli was a good man. He was a good dad. He cared for his son Dominick dearly. But Eli had a problem. His son made very poor choices when he was out on the streets with his friends. And Eli didn't know what to do. He would try talking to his son, but nothing would get through. Over time, his son's decisions became increasingly erratic. And the consequences for those decisions became increasingly serious. Eli felt powerless and afraid for his son.

Although, Eli was not the kind of man to take things lying down. He was not going to let his son throw away his life without a fight. So, he fought son with his words. He said and did whatever it took to shock his son into reality. He called him "dumb," "stupid," "idiotic," and "infantile."

Eli was willing to say and do anything to get his son's attention. After several months of trying this tactic, his son's behavior only worsened. Dominick's *poor* choices became *rebellious* choices. His choices were meant to spite his dad. He felt hurt by his dad's words, so he was going to hurt his dad back. As you can imagine, the tension in their relationship escalated. Enter stage right, me.

When I started working with the family, Eli asked me some very pointed questions. Why can't I get through to my son? Why is he getting worse? I shared with Eli that regardless of his intent, which I believed was good, his parenting strategy was shame-based and shaming comes with serious backfires. Dad's choice of words, tone, body language and general demeanor was one of mockery, disgust, disrespect and accusation. I stated very clearly that I understood Eli's heart was in the right place. He was trying anything to get through to his son. But, he needed to pay attention to the results of his words. The results were clear. Shaming backfired, time and time again.

This puzzled Eli. I shared with him that shaming tends to have the opposite effect than what we, as parents, intend. When Eli tries to influence his son, but shame is present, Dominick feels attacked. When Eli tries to help Dominick think about his actions, but shame is present, Dominick feels embarrassed. When Eli tries to instruct Dominick, but shame is present, Dominick feels talked down to.

I asked Eli if he'd be willing to consider alternative methods to achieving his goal, since, what he'd been doing up to this point hadn't worked. He was hesitant, but willing to hear me out. I told him that *if he wanted the same results, then keep doing the same thing*. But, *if he wanted different results, he needed to try something different.* And that different thing I suggested was to *stop* shaming his son. And to *start* building up a relationship where his son feels safe to share honestly with his dad. And, when dad wants to give his son instruction, he needs to make sure that he son feels loved and supported by his dad. I said, when Dominick feels this from dad, he will be more open to what dad has to say.

I also stated that ultimately dad should want his son to think through problems critically, to arrive at an intelligent solution, and take responsible action on his own. It is not a problem when Dominick seeks help from dad, but, dad ultimately wants his son to be able to do this on his own. So, dad needed to shift positions from being *the sage on the stage, to the guide on the side.*

I walked him through the various tools introduced in this chapter. I told him these were methods of influence that don't backfire. It took dad some time, but he came around and dropped his shaming tactics and started using other means to influence his son in a more positive and effective manner. Their relationship improved as a result and Dominick felt more comfortable approaching dad with what was really going on in his life. In Dominick's eyes, dad became an ally instead of an adversary.

Eli and Dominick are not a special case. They are the average, run of the mill dad and son duo. They are not special people, but they were able to accomplish special outcomes. And this was done by stopping shame and starting positive means of influence. Dad didn't shy away from having hard conversations with his son, but his approach wasn't laced with shame. And that translated into better outcomes. Outcomes that you can experience too, when you drop shame from your parenting.

Epilogue

The journey of a thousand miles begins with a single step.
—Lao Tzu

This may have been a hard read for you. It's not easy to take a critical look at yourself, but sometimes an honest look in the mirror is exactly what you need. Think about it. The thing that you are so protective of, your parenting, is also protecting you from growth.

If you never tear off the Band-Aid, you'll never get help. Tear the Band-Aid off and look at what's under there. It will give you a picture of what's wrong and how to fix it.

Change is hard, especially when it comes to your parenting practices. But are you willing to hurt your parenting and relationship with your kids at the expense of protecting your ego? If you're reading this book, I don't think you are. You cared enough about your kids to read this book. That's a start. That's a first step. The nice thing about taking the first step is that subsequent steps get easier. You can't fix everything at once, but you can start with one thing. Take the second step and apply some of the concepts mentioned in this book to your parenting.

About the Authors

For fifteen years, David Simonsen has been helping people work through challenges in their lives. This experience has given him the ability to get to the source(s) of the challenges quickly and efficiently. He uses humor and directness to help people get back on track in their relationships. He has a passion for helping teens and parents connect. David has his PhD in psychology and an MS in marriage and family therapy. He has been married for eighteen years and has seven kids.

Daniel Bates is a Licensed Mental Health Counselor and is a Nationally Certified Counselor based out of Vancouver, Washington. He loves all things psychology and mental health. Aside from his work with families in the justice system and his work with clients in his private practice, he wants to bring the life-changing insights from the field of psychology to public through his podcast, *Counselor Dan Podcast*, through books, through his blog and through YouTube videos. This content can be found on his website, counselordan.com. He weekly delivers unique content to his blog, posts a new podcast episode and adds videos to his YouTube channel, *Counselor Dan Videos*. There are many ways to follow Daniel by subscribing to his blog, or his podcast available on iTunes and Podbean, or on his YouTube channel.

More from Daniel Bates

Family Crisis Guidebook: Practical Steps to Work through Difficult Situations

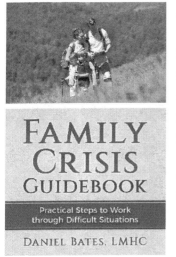

Family Crisis Guidebook will help you and your family navigate through a relational, addiction and or mental health crisis in ways that will not only help you out of a bad situation, but will help your family achieve sustained change. Change is the only true antidote to future crises.

Family Crisis Guidebook will help you and your family learn how to:

- Properly understand the crisis
- Change dysfunctional patterns of behavior
- Create new and healthy patterns of behavior
- Practical skills for everyone in the family
- Maintain lasting, sustained change that will buffer you from future crises and help your family grow in ways you haven't imagined.

Crises can be scary and overwhelming, especially when they concern people you love, but denial is not an option. *Family Crisis Guidebook* can help you do just that by successfully guiding back on the right path.

The Modern Mystic

Wish your spiritual life wasn't mediocre? Is your prayer life dead? Are you jealous of the spiritual vitality that everyone else seems to have except for you? Don't let your life be ruled by a spiritual malaise. Instead of checking out, go further and deeper in to the heart of God.

But how?

The Christian mystics are ancient voices with a modern message. They teach that the love of God is deeper, wider and beyond anything you can understand. It is altogether mysterious and right in front of you. It is the paradoxical truth wrapped in the unimaginable love of a relational God eager to know and be known by you.

Yes, you are the object of God's love. And yes, God is the ultimate source of your happiness. Knowing and experiencing God's love will change you. Yet experiencing God's love is not a destination. It is a journey. And you are a sojourner in need of a guide. Allow the Christian mystics to direct you along the sometimes-confusing wandering path of God's love.

Learning to Live

You are the reason you are stuck. You can either stay stuck or learn how to get un-stuck. In order to get un-stuck, you must engage in the learning process. That means learning about yourself, your perceptions, your thinking, your communication style, and how you view relationships. But learning is hard to do with some help. Fortunately, an experienced therapist, Daniel Bates, has compiled 20 lessons based on his clinical experience and the latest social science research to help you.

Learning to Live will help you engage with the lifelong work of learning. Learning isn't an event, it's a journey. It can be painful, challenging at times and downright uncomfortable, but the end result is worth it. Lessons have a way of sticking with you for the rest of your life. They are the gift that keeps on giving. So, what are you waiting for? Start learning so you can start living.

Even a Superhero Needs Counseling

This book provides an in-depth guide to understanding your favorite comic book character from a psychological perspective while providing you with relevant and insightful advice. In other words, by learning more about Thor, the Hulk, Wonder Woman, Stephen Strange, Superman and many more, you can learn more about yourself. Comic books aren't just entertainment; they can be a window into the strengths and weaknesses of humanity. In each chapter, you'll find:

An overview of major comic book character's origin story, arch-enemies, and dynamics of their psychology.

A mental health diagnosis based on the relevant details of the character's symptoms.

What mental health treatment would consist of based on the diagnosis and how it would help their life.

And, most importantly, how your favorite comic book character's story can be informative for you own personal growth.

Whatever the problem, you will find a superhero or supervillain that shares your struggle. And it is through their stories, you can find help for yours.

Daniel's Podcast

Counselor Dan Podcast is a podcast for those who want to be entertained and informed. The podcast goes deep into the latest research from psychology, surveys fascinating insights from field of counseling, and delves into the personal experiences Daniel has accrued over his career. You can find Counselor Dan Podcast at counselordanpodcast.com, or on Daniels' website, counselordan.com, it is also available on iTunes, Podbean and other podcast hosting sites.

Daniel's Website

Daniel's blog, videos, books, and information about counseling services can be found on his website, counselordan.com. The website is a one-stop shop for all of Daniel's content. Weekly he posts new podcasts, unique content to his blog, and videos to his YouTube page all available on the website. You can also learn more about Daniel's books and find out where to purchase them. And, learn more about his counseling practice if you are looking for further mental health support.

Counseling Services

If you are interested contacting Daniel for counseling, he recently expanded his private practice at Lacamas Counseling in Camas, Washington. You can find information about Daniel's counseling specialties, location of the office or other counselors that may be a fit for you at lacamascounseling.com. He's currently accepting new clients. Email or Call to schedule an appointment.

38966810R00088

Made in the USA
Middletown, DE
14 March 2019